ant **expert** ● instant **expert** ● instant **expert** ● instant **expert** ●

PAINT
EFFECTS

Thunder Bay Press
An imprint of the Advantage Publishers Group
THUNDER BAY 5880 Oberlin Drive, San Diego, CA 92121-4794
P·R·E·S·S www.thunderbaybooks.com

Copyright © MQ Publications 2005
Text copyright © Hilary Mandleberg 2005

Series Editor: Katy Bevan, MQ Publications
Editorial Director: Ljiljana Baird, MQ Publications
Photography: Steve Tanner
Styling: Katy Bevan
Design concept: Balley Design Associates

All notations of errors or omissions should be addressed to Thunder Bay
Press, Editorial Department, at the above address. All other
correspondence (author inquiries, permissions) concerning the content of
this book should be addressed to MQ Publications,
12 The Ivories, 6-8 Northampton Street, London N1 2HY, England.

ISBN-13: 978-1-59223-420-2
ISBN-10: 1-59223-420-8

Printed in China
1 2 3 4 5 09 08 07 06 05

Library of Congress Cataloging-in-Publication Data

Mandleberg, Hilary.
    Paint effects / Hilary Mandleberg.
       p. cm. -- (Instant expert)
    Includes index.
     ISBN 1-59223-420-8 (hardcover)
      1. Painting--Technique. 2. Decoration and ornament. I. Title. II. Instant expert (Thunder
Bay Press)

   TT385.M363 2005
   747'.3--dc22

                                                          2005044039

instant **expert** • instant **expert** • instant **expert** •

PAINT EFFECTS

hilary mandleberg

THUNDER BAY
P·R·E·S·S

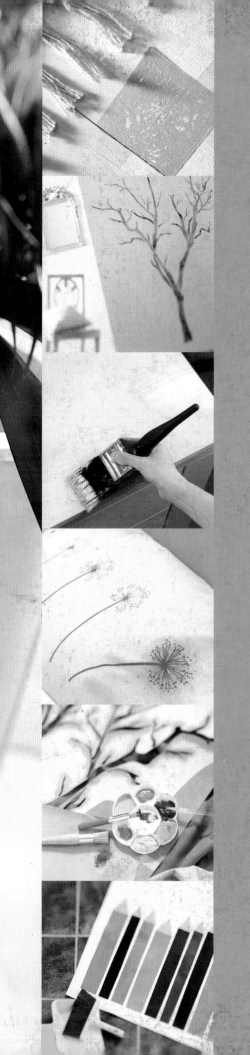

Contents

INTRODUCTION

When my children were young, I took the greatest pleasure in decorating their nursery. I made a stenciled valance based on a couple of the animals that were featured in the drapes, I decorated the floor tiles for indoor hopscotch, and I stenciled letters of the alphabet on the lid of their toy chest. When they became older, one child's bedroom had sponged walls and the other had a leaf design stamp.

I am glad to say that paint effects are still with us and are, in fact, enjoying something of a revival. People have realized that they offer a satisfying outlet for their creativity, at the same time enhancing their home by adding designer touches at a fraction of the cost.

This book offers a wide range of paint effects projects, all with easy-to-follow step-by-step instructions. They are divided into three sections— Stamping and Stenciling, Free and Easy, and Texture and Shine, each beginning with an overview of the techniques required. The projects are suitable for all abilities, from complete beginners to experienced and confident painters. What is more, there are projects for every room and surface in the home— for floors, walls, tiles, plates, floorcloths, vases, drapes, picture frames, furniture, and even bed linen.

The materials you require will, of course, vary according to the size of your particular project. I have given the quantities used for the projects as shown here, together with their measurements.

I hope you will enjoy the projects in this book, and I am sure that you will feel inspired to use the techniques you learn here to design many more projects of your own.

Opposite: The motifs and technique used on these flowerpots to add color and textural interest were inspired by the pre-Columbian art of Mexico.

part

1

A HISTORY OF PAINT EFFECTS

A HISTORY OF PAINT EFFECTS

In the beginning there was … a blank surface, but it wasn't long before someone somewhere had the idea of decorating it. And so the art of decoration began. Just as nature abhors a vacuum, so human beings seem to abhor a blank surface.

For example, how often have you sat in a meeting and started doodling on a piece of paper, or doodled on the telephone message pad while you were on the phone? What about the fencing that builders put up around a building site only to come to work the next day to find that, overnight, the bare fence has inexplicably been covered with graffiti? Even in this exciting technological age, that same urge exists: why else would we cover our blank computer screen with a screensaver?

Cave art

Thanks to present-day technology, when we feel like a change of scene at our computer, a simple click of a mouse button will do the job. Wizardry like this wasn't possible for our ancestors the cavemen, though. Once they had decorated the walls of their caves, that was that. And thank heaven for it, as we can now gaze in wonder at cave paintings that date back many thousands of years. In France, for example, there are paintings in the caves of the Ardèche that are thought to be 30,000 years old, while the renowned paintings at Lascaux in the Périgord are estimated to be 15,000 years old. Then there are the equally famous paintings, believed to have been carried out between 11,000 and 19,000 years ago, located deep in the recesses of the caves at Altamira in northern Spain and, in the year 2000, what may be the world's oldest known cave paintings—possibly between 32,000 and 36,500 years old—were discovered in northern Italy.

Moving beyond Europe, there are cave paintings in Bhimabetaka near Bhopal in India that may be 20,000 years old, as well as the San or bushmen paintings that are preserved at the Game Pass Shelter in the Ukhahlamba Drakensberg Park in South Africa and that are thought to have been made over a period of 4,000 years. The thousand-year-old cave paintings of Baja, California, and the 30,000 Saharan cave paintings of the Tassili plateau, date from the end of the sixth to the middle of the fourth millennium. In Australia, more than 100,000 rock art sites have been discovered, including the 4,000-year-old aboriginal site discovered at Eagles Reach in May 2003.

The very earliest rock art consisted of rock carvings, but all the sites mentioned above have an array of painted scenes that largely feature animals, and sometimes humans involved in domestic scenes. For example, the cave paintings of the Tassili plateau are mostly of animals—oversized rhinos and elephants, giraffes, gazelles, camels, ostriches, and hares. The animals have a variety of hides, some mottled, some plain, and they also have a variety of horn types. The domestic scenes show women cooking and drawing water, men splitting wood with axes, children sleeping, women harvesting, musicians, dancers, and, dating from 1000 BC, battles with neighboring peoples.

Although it is not certain why these primitive people painted such scenes, it is obvious that they were an important part of their culture and not merely adornment for their living quarters. Indeed, cave people mostly lived in readily accessible caves on the rock face, while most of these cave paintings have been found in deeper caves, and often in inaccessible places such as very high up the wall or on a high ceiling, suggesting that a lot of time was spent on their painting and that they must, therefore, have been very significant. In fact, many scholars believe that even all those thousands of years ago, certain people in the tribal group were designated as artists and may even have worked with a team of helpers—people to help them build scaffolding for reaching the most inaccessible stretches of wall, others to mix paints, yet others to make the lamps for them to work by in the dark, and so on.

As hunter-gatherers gave way to cultivators, people

Opposite: Cave paintings of animals being hunted at Marmar Tassili in the Tibesti Mountains, Sahara Desert, Chad.

became more settled in their lives. They started to build permanent homes for themselves, and towns and villages sprang up with buildings designated for special purposes such as temples, shops, and tombs, as well as homes for the rulers and the noble classes and the more modest homes of the ordinary people.

Ancient civilizations

Ancient Egypt is one of the best known of the ancient civilizations, offering myriad examples of the different ways artists used painted decoration. We can still visit and be amazed by their temples and by the tombs of royalty and nobility, whose walls were completely covered with carved and painted inscriptions describing the life and afterlife of gods and princes. The wooden mummy cases found in the tombs were elaborately painted with cartouches bearing the names of the deceased, along with images of his or her journey to the underworld and prayers for their safe passage. And to see them on their way, there were the grave goods—objects like the beautiful painted, gilded, and inlaid wooden chests, beds, and couches found in the spectacular tomb of Tutankhamen, and dating from around

Above: A school of dolphins decorate a wall from ca. 1500 BC in the queen's apartment at Knossos on Crete.

1300 BC. From these and other finds, we know that ancient Egyptian artists were well acquainted with emulating the materials of the natural world, and as early as the third dynasty were competent with techniques like wood graining—painting one wood to look like a more expensive one.

Another famous ancient civilization that used decorative painting was that of the Minoans who lived on the island of Crete during the Bronze Age. Their palace in the capital, Knossos, was built in 2000–1350 BC and is renowned for its beautiful frescoes (now heavily restored) of dolphins, bull-jumping, and scenes of dancing. The Mycaeneans, who held sway on the Greek mainland at roughly the same time, liked similar, heavily decorated wall surfaces, but their motifs were more often human beings than nature scenes.

The city-states of ancient Greece that followed the Mycaeneans are not especially known for their use of painted decoration, but this is largely because much of it has been lost over time. We look at the Parthenon in Athens and only see the beautiful, aged, creamy-white marble of its pillars and carvings, yet when it was first built, it was covered with painted decoration in bright reds, blues, greens, and gold that we can only guess at today from the faint traces that remain. If we need proof of their expertise in the art of painting, though, we only have to look at the quality of painting on Greek vases and bowls.

When it comes to the Romans, we have far more evidence of their love of painted decoration. Our main sources of information are, of course, the ruins of Pompeii and Herculaneum, the two towns destroyed in a matter of hours during the eruption of Mount Vesuvius in AD 79. Here we can still see, preserved for posterity by layer upon layer of ash, evidence of shops and even brothels advertising their wares by means of wall paintings. More privately, there are entire houses with frescoed walls depicting scenes from mythology and from secret rites and rituals. Here, too, is evidence of early forms of faux painting—plastered walls are divided with trompe l'oeil columns and architraves framing imaginary scenes; bare plaster is painted to mimic marble and other stones. All of this provided a rich seam to be tapped centuries later during the Renaissance, when artists looked to the classical past for inspiration.

At about the same time as the Romans ruled the ancient world, the new world was developing a huge and powerful center at Teotihuacán in Mexico which, by AD 200, boasted about 60,000–80,000 inhabitants. The name Teotihuacán means "place of the gods," and this enormous pyramid complex thirty miles northeast of Mexico City was one of the most splendid civilizations of ancient America. The art of the fresco was one of its specialties. At the Temple of Quetzalcoatl (the Temple of the Feathered Serpent) the frescoed walls show processions of priests, gods, and allegorical animals all painted in reds, greens, blues, and yellows that are still bright today. In the Tepantitla complex is the Paradise of Tlaloc, a fresco showing the afterlife of men who died of causes relating to rain or water (Tlaloc was the Great Earth-Water Goddess). These men are represented as happy figures, dancing, playing games, and chasing butterflies.

Below: The highly decorated painted walls that surround the tomb of Tutankhamen in Luxor, Egypt.

A few hundred years later, around AD 800, the Mayans built Bonampak in modern-day Chiapas in Mexico. Discovered in 1946, this has some of the best-preserved color murals of any Maya site, depicting various rituals, ceremonial processions, a raid on a neighboring village, and the punishment of prisoners.

Europe and the Renaissance

Returning to Europe, and we are in the Dark Ages, the period of history between the fall of the Roman Empire and the Renaissance. This was a time when the arts were largely dominated by the Church, and most artists were employed either by the Church or by kings and queens and the nobility. Painting was a major art form, though it often took the shape of portable paintings to hang in churches or palaces, but many churches also were decorated with beautiful frescoes. At the same time, wood and plaster carvings were often gilded to make them look like solid gold, and faux marble and faux wood were sometimes used to cut construction costs.

Looking eastward, in Russia, the Cathedral of the Assumption is the Kremlin's oldest and most important church. The seat of Russian Orthodoxy was transferred here from Vladimir in 1326. Its spacious, light interior is entirely covered with glowing frescoes, originally created by the famous icon painter Dionysius and his team of artists but later restored in the 1640s and once again in Soviet times. It is a sight to behold and a wonder of the fresco artist's skills.

With the Renaissance in Italy, the art of fresco painting reached new heights. In the fourteenth century, during the very early Renaissance, Giotto proved to be a revolutionary master of the art. His frescoes, carried out in the space of only two years between 1303 and 1305 in the vaulted Scrovegni Chapel in Padua, are sublime, with hundreds of real gold-leaf stars scattered across the deep blue ceiling. His paintings, which depict more than a hundred Bible scenes, completely cover the 900 square yards of the 700-year-old Scrovegni Chapel's walls and ceiling.

Moving on a little more than a hundred years to the early Renaissance, Fra Angelico was a friar whose Dominican order took over the convent of San Marco in 1436. He was commissioned to decorate the friar's cells with frescoes painted directly onto the wet plaster walls. Piero della Francesca was yet another exponent of the art of fresco

Below: A detail of *The Marriage at Cana*, part of the fresco painted by Giotto in 1303–1305 in the Scrovegni Chapel, Padua, Italy.

painting during the early Renaissance, with his images of the *Discovery and Proof of the True Cross* dating from around 1466 at the Church of San Francesco in Arezzo. Raphael was yet another star in the fresco painter firmament. A contemporary of Michelangelo, he painted the work of art known as *The School of Athens* in the Vatican at the same time as Michelangelo was there painting the frescoes of the Sistine Chapel. Two greats under one roof!

Meanwhile, away from the Church, in the homes of the wealthy, the cult of the Renaissance and its emulation of all things classical took hold. The demand grew for stone walls, pillars, classical sculpture, and carved lettering, and if you could not afford the real thing, then why not have an artist paint it for you? This was the next big moment in decorative painting, and the refinement of painting techniques improved by leaps and bounds. The imitation of marble slabs, together with their joints, was the height of fashion for walls; porphyry, lapis lazuli, and other semiprecious stones were emulated in paint on furniture, while trompe l'oeil mimicked classical swags, moldings, sculpture, lettering—even entire scenes of people leaning over balustrades or walking through doors.

As a middle class developed, its members sought to emulate the better off. For instance, in Italy, it became the fashion for merchants to commission artists to paint "wall hangings" for their homes, to mimic the opulent wall hangings they had seen on their travels and that only the upper classes could afford to buy. With the opening up of the Silk Route for trade with countries as far-flung as China, there was suddenly a new range of products to be emulated in paint—tortoiseshell, mother-of-pearl, and exotic woods, for instance.

The impact of France

Louis XIV, France's Sun King, had the longest reign in European history (1643–1715). During this time, he brought absolute monarchy to its height, established a glittering court at Versailles, and fought most of the other European countries in four wars. No wonder, then, that the magnificent palace of Versailles, a jewel of baroque architecture that Louis built to escape from Paris, and to which he moved his court in 1682, was to have such an impact on the European art scene.

Louis employed the most talented craftsmen of his day and had the finest materials brought to this village not far from Paris in order to create, from nothing more than the hunting lodge used by his father, the most magnificent palace Europe had ever seen. He had it adorned with marble and semiprecious stones, fine plasterwork, the most expensive woods, gold and silver leaf, mirror, tapestries, paintings, silk hangings, the finest porcelain and furniture—everything that money could buy.

Louis XV, who ruled from 1715 to 1744, and Louis XVI, who ruled from 1744 to 1792, continued the work started by their father and grandfather. Over the years, the Palace of Versailles also became a showcase for the rococo and neoclassical styles that were to follow Louis XIV's baroque.

All the monarchs of Europe turned to Versailles for inspiration for their palaces, but perhaps none did so with more aplomb than Gustav III of Sweden, who ruled as a semiabsolute monarch from 1771 to 1792 and who gave his name to what has come to be called "Gustavian" style. In effect, this was an adaptation of French style to suit the more austere Swedish taste and the less well endowed Swedish purse of the eighteenth century. Furniture was modeled on imported furniture, but its lines were simplified so they could be copied by provincial craftsmen. And because the Swedes could not afford expensive woods for their furniture, they painted it instead, using a palette of soft grays, blues, and off-whites. When it came to the walls, painted canvases mimicked wood paneling and precious silks, and pine replaced oak parquet on the floors.

But before this, in 1728, after a break of twenty years, work had started again on the Royal Palace in Stockholm. Artists and craftsmen were brought in from Paris to ensure that the most up-to-date styles and materials were used. By the middle of the 1730s, wealthy Swedes were importing such large quantities of furniture, fabrics, ornaments, and wall coverings to decorate their homes in the French style, that the state set up a manufacturing office in 1739 to support Swedish manufacture. In 1745, Jean Eric Rehn was appointed its artistic director. He had studied in Paris, and he returned there regularly to keep in touch with the latest trends.

Meanwhile, Jean-François de Neufforge's *Recueil Elémentaire d'Architecture* was published in installments between 1757 and 1770, and, using its pages as his inspiration, Rehn created, in the Grand Salon of the manor house at Sturefors, what retrospectively can be called the first Gustavian room, with its linen-covered walls painted to look like marble, its faux niches, its molded frames around portrait medallions, and its gilded allegorical sculptures.

The Gustavian style proved to be a blend of rococo and the more restrained classicism. It suited the Swedes perfectly. As well as using paint techniques to emulate marble, plasterwork, silk, and tapestry, painted borders of Greek key designs, laurel leaves, and floral swags proved popular, and these were often used to surround painted linen or canvas wall panels that could be changed from time to time.

Gustavian taste spread quickly, and Swedish artists who had trained under the French craftsmen who worked on the Royal Palace were in great demand. Gradually the style filtered down through society, and it was no longer just the aristocrats who wanted the look in their homes.

England and the colonies

It wasn't only in Sweden that faux paint effects took hold. In England from the seventeenth to early nineteenth century, it was believed that a considerable part of a painter's skill lay in the imitation of fine materials, such as the imitation of marble, cabinet timbers, bronze, tortoiseshell, and mother-of-pearl. When the cornices of some of the rooms at Dover Castle were painted in 1625–1626, they were described as being done "like stoneworke in distemper."

Sometimes timber, both interior and exterior, was "sanded" to look like stone; in other words, sand was dusted onto the wet paint. This technique was used in the Great Hall at Bowood House in Wiltshire in 1765 and in the mid-1790s at Frogmore House in the private Home Park of Windsor Castle, Berkshire.

By the late seventeenth century, the imitation of tortoiseshell inlay was popular for mirror frames, and Christopher Wren used the technique for the columns and friezes of the altarpiece in the Tudor Chapel in Whitehall Palace, London, in 1676.

Also in the late seventeenth century and onward, metal powder was used to imitate lacquerwork, and by the end of the eighteenth century in England, doors and trim were decorated in an imitation of green-patinated bronze, with other bronzing colors used on plaster, iron, and lead.

Even mother-of-pearl was imitated. The technique involved using a background similar to that used for wood graining. The motifs were then sketched on, and silver leaf applied, with red, blue, and yellow pigments painted on and manipulated to achieve the desired effect.

Meanwhile, taste was not much different in America. Wealthy Americans watched English styles closely and either traveled to England, returning with household goods, or ordered them through London suppliers.

By the end of the seventeenth century, painted decoration on furniture was popular in America, as we know from the records of a firm in Connecticut that produced chests painted with either floral or geometric designs. Painted furniture was prominent in New York interiors: wood graining to imitate richer woods was popular, as were simple chairs painted in solid colors.

Painted wallpapers were even beginning to make their way to the colonies. In 1700, some wallpaper was listed in the inventory of possessions of a certain Michael Perry who died in Boston, but wallpapers were not actually produced in America until 1739 when the first wallpaper shop opened its doors in Philadelphia.

It has long been assumed that it took ten years for English styles to reach America, but that was not necessarily the case. During the reign of Queen Anne (1715–1750), the wealthy were very good at keeping up with fashions on the other side of the Atlantic. One Boston merchant had frescoes painted in his home in 1712, others had landscapes and coats of arms on their walls, and a house in Rhode Island in 1740 boasted frescoes in a chinoiserie design.

The first painted floorcloth arrived in Virginia in 1739, and floorboards were sometimes painted with geometric or leaf decorations, with pumpkin yellow, gray, and brown being common colors. We have a record of the fact that Indian red was a good color for a floor, too, but it apparently required quite a lot of upkeep.

While Thomas Chippendale held sway in England (1750–1810), the new English rococo style was gradually established in wealthy American homes. Until this period, plastered walls had simply been limewashed, but, gradually, as the palette of available colors increased, painted walls became more fashionable.

Painted floorcloths continued to be popular and were sometimes used as a substitute for heavier carpets, often as a washable protection over another carpet beneath the dining table. John Carwithen's *Floor Decoration for Various Kinds*, of 1739, offered patterns for floorcloths that included marbling, together with geometric shapes, especially square and

Above: Paint imitates an exotic scene in these trompe l'oeil frescoes by Paolo Veronese, in the Villa Barbaro in Venice, Italy.

diamond motifs. There were even some patterns that imitated Wilton or Turkey carpets.

In this same period, Pennsylvania German variants began to appear, which perhaps bore more relation to rural paint technique developments in Europe (firmly rooted in the vernacular, and in a strong, vivacious style and bold colors) than to mainstream American styles. The first German colonists had arrived in Pennsylvania in 1683, and thousands more came in the eighteenth century. They favored color combinations such as white walls with blue trim, or furniture painted in reds and blue-greens. They also loved to decorate benches and chests with motifs of painted hearts, unicorns, grapes, tulips, and leaves. One of their specialties was the bridal chest, which appeared with distinct patterns according to the region where it was produced.

America breaks away

The federal style in America, from 1785 to 1815, was epitomized by the innovative neoclassical work of Scottish architect Robert Adam. The style came to America by way of British pattern books and an ever-swelling wave of immigrant masons, carpenters, and joiners.

Paint effects were now at their height, and itinerant painters and decorators had plenty of work. They traveled the country stenciling borders at ceiling height, above chair rails, and in corners, or covering walls in bold, allover stenciled patterns of flowers, vines, urns, and the federal eagle. In homes where the owner was a devotee of Freemasonry, they might stencil compass points around the walls of the room used for lodge meetings, or they might be asked, as one decorator was, to produce a dark blue, star-studded ceiling with the "all-seeing eye" in the center. A variant of this, the clouded ceiling, was also popular both in America and in England during this period.

When stenciling was not called for, the decorator might be commissioned to hand-paint the walls of a room, an option that was dearer than stenciling but less costly than wallpaper. Seascapes were popular, while at Abel Griswold House in Windsor, Connecticut, the trompe l'oeil paneling was no doubt the owner's pride and joy.

Meanwhile, in Britain, D.R. Hay of Edinburgh patented a method for imitating damask in paint, and he published two processes for achieving this. He also devised a similar technique for emulating gold brocade.

At the same time, techniques for graining had improved considerably, and, thanks to technical advances in the use of glazes, graining was an important decorative technique in the early part of the nineteenth century. It was usually varnished to give the appearance of the depth of polished timber.

The nineteenth century

The empire period (1810–1830) in America brought some changes, but not many. In the country, eighteenth-century style persisted, while in towns and cities people largely kept up with developments in Europe, replacing their stenciled walls with wall painting that imitated the designs of expensive French wallpapers.

Floorcloths, still in use to protect dining-room carpets, continued the art of imitation, but painted floors were becoming rarer. However, one floor of 1830 in New Hampshire was painted to look like striped carpet.

The so-called Victorian classical period in America lasted from 1830 until 1850 and was a rich era for painted furniture in country areas. Painted classical motifs were popular. For example, pillar and scroll motifs, and graining and marbling were still to be found. In fact, by the end of this period, graining had reached new heights: in England, Bolton grainer Thomas Kershaw claimed to be able to grain slate to make it look like oak, and oak to look like marble—no mean feat!

But as the century drew to a close, the fashion for paint effects waned. The industrial revolution had brought mass production, and there was no longer room in people's lives for painstakingly worked, expensive paint trickery. Art Nouveau and Japonisme were popular artistic trends, but, apart from having an influence on wallpaper designs of the time, their main influence was in the realms of metalwork, furniture and woodwork, glassware, jewelry, painting, and poster design.

Disciples of the arts and crafts movement rebelled against mass production and sought a return to handicrafts, old values, and vernacular styles. Following the precepts of their leader William Morris (1834–1896), they did not care for unnecessary ornament but instead preferred the natural grain and color of wood to show, and for walls to be painted white, or papered with one of Morris & Co.'s very fashionable stylized floral wallpapers. Morris told his followers to have "nothing in your houses that you do not know to be useful." Paint effects were clearly passé.

The twentieth century

The years before World War I were some of the most daring and adventurous in the world of art, but, in general, this failed to trickle through into people's homes. One of the most significant influences of the time in domestic interiors was the Scottish designer and architect Charles Rennie Mackintosh, who blended the flourishes of Art Nouveau with the simplicity of Japonisme. Thanks to him, there arose a fashion for white-painted furniture and for stylized flower motifs, often used as wall stencils.

Meanwhile, another flourish of activity was taking place at Charleston, an old house in Sussex, England, to which the artists Vanessa Bell and Duncan Grant had moved with their unconventional household in 1916. Over the following half century, Charleston became the country meeting place for the group of artists, writers, and intellectuals known as the Bloomsbury set. Seeking to rebel against the increasing mechanization of the age and the realities of a world being destroyed by war, and inspired by Italian fresco painting and the post-impressionists, Bell and Grant proceeded to decorate the walls, doors, and furniture at Charleston with primitive vibrancy. The house was restored and opened to the public in the 1980s. At that time, there was the start of a revival of interest in paint effects.

Since then there has been no stopping the interest in paint effects for the home, and people have been marbleizing, stenciling, stamping, patinating, and graining to their hearts' content. They are part of a great tradition. Long may it last!

Left: The washstand in the spare bedroom at Charleston, the home of some of the Bloomsbury set in Sussex, England, was probably decorated by Duncan Grant in 1946. The window was decorated by Vanessa Bell ten years earlier.

citronella

sweet violet

winchester Red

Canary

Fern Green

Happy violet

5

nea

part

2

BEFORE YOU START

COLOR

When you are deciding on a paint effect for your home, you not only have to think about the design you want, but also about the color you will use, and this can be daunting. It always seems as if the artistic geniuses of the past had an instinct for the right color in the right place.

The same is true when we flip through magazines and books on interior design. We ask ourselves how the interior designer or stylist managed to get the colors just right. Well, the truth is that they may actually have struggled a bit. Michelangelo may have made a few attempts at the colors of Adam in the Sistine Chapel before he felt truly happy with what he had done, and the interior designer would doubtless have tried out many color combinations on a swatch board (see page 32), before deciding which one looked best.

The reason is that color is a very complicated subject. As you know, where there is no light, we don't see any color. You may also have noticed that the way we see color depends on the quality of the light. It also depends on which other colors are nearby. And, so it is said, no two people see the same color in exactly the same way. So where do we begin?

The science of color

In 1666, Isaac Newton passed a ray of light through a prism of glass and saw that it was broken up into a series of bands of different colors—red, orange, yellow, green, blue, and violet. In other words, white light actually consists of all these colors—the colors of the spectrum—blended together, and between them is an indefinite number of intermediate colors. As was later discovered, each color of the spectrum emits a different wavelength.

But how do we see the colors? The answer lies in the fact that every object absorbs some parts of the spectrum and reflects others, so when we look at something, the retina of the eye, which is sensitive to light wavelengths, picks up the wavelengths that are being reflected by the object and sends a message to our brain telling us what color we can see.

Right: A color wheel is a traditional way of presenting color.
Opposite: Fields of tulips growing in the Netherlands are the epitome of color in nature.

Classifying color

The science of color is all very well, but when it comes to the practicality of choosing a color scheme for your paint effect, it may not seem to help much. But that is only an illusion. Knowing about the colors of the spectrum helps us understand how color is classified, and that helps us see why some colors work well together and others do not.

The first thing to know is that among the colors of the spectrum are the three primary colors—red, blue, and yellow. These cannot be made from any other colors, but, in theory, all other colors can be made from them. Then there are the secondary colors of the spectrum—green (made from blue and yellow), orange (made from red and yellow), and violet (made from blue and red). If you mix two secondaries together, you will get the tertiaries—violet and orange make russet, orange and green make citron, and violet and green make olive.

A color wheel will take you a step further. It arranges the colors of the spectrum in a circle, with the three primary

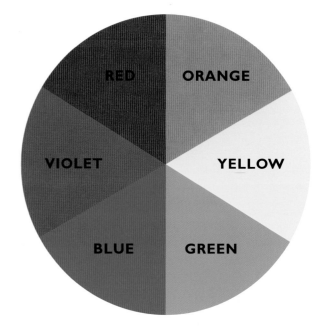

colors appearing with their secondaries between them and, in more complicated color wheels, with the tertiaries between the secondaries.

Generally speaking, you can take any cluster of adjoining colors from the wheel and use them together successfully. That is because they harmonize with one another, the reason being that they each contain elements of one another. So an orange-red, made from mixing red with yellow, will appear harmonious with the red and yellow from which it is made and with any other colors made from that red or yellow.

Now look at colors that are opposite each other on the color wheel. These are known as complementary colors. Put them together and you will have a contrast. So red is directly opposite green on the wheel, and blue is opposite orange. These contrasts can work well together, but they are much more challenging than harmonious combinations.

Tints, shades, and tone

But that is not the entire story. You may have noticed that the color wheel does not include every color under the sun. What it is lacking are the tints and shades. These are made by adding white—in the case of a tint—or black—in

the case of a shade. In other words, these are lighter and darker colors of the original. Pink is a tint of red and mustard is a shade of yellow. In general, a collection of tints based on the same primary will all look good—or harmonious—together, as will a collection of shades.

Another aspect of color, but one which many people find hard to grasp, is the concept of tone. This is the degree of lightness or darkness of a color compared to black or white. The most extreme contrast of tone is, in fact, the contrast between black and white. On the other hand, some reds and greens are so tonally similar that when they are next to each other, we are not aware of any tonal contrast between them. When you are planning your paint effect, choose colors that are tonally similar for greater harmony and colors that have more tonal difference for a greater contrast.

Color "temperature"

One other thing to be aware of—and you can see it remarkably clearly when you look at the color wheel— is that some colors are "warm" while others are "cool." On the color wheel, the cool colors are opposite the warm ones. When it comes to choosing color for a room, the "temperature" of the color can make an enormous difference. For one thing, cool colors appear to recede and warm colors advance, so a cool blue painted on one wall of a room has the effect of making the room feel longer, while the same wall painted in a warm orange will make the room feel more compact.

If you take this idea and run with it, you will see how using cool colors will make a space feel calmer and more spacious while using warm colors will make it feel cozier. You can also use this fact to enhance a room's atmosphere if you wish. So if you have a small, cozy room and you want it to feel that way, have the courage of your convictions and decorate it with warm colors.

Color "temperature" is also important if you choose to mix your own paint colors. Do you have a red that feels too hot? If so, cool it down by adding a touch of blue. If that green is too cool, then warm it up with a dab of yellow. Now add in some white and black, and the sky's the limit— you can have any color you want.

Left: This harmonious bedroom is based on shades of beige. The result is calm and soothing, and nothing jars.

Color and texture

Every surface has its own inherent texture: normal window glass is completely smooth, but frosted glass is often used for a bathroom window. There is smooth stainless steel for a kitchen backsplash, and textured metal for the floor. You may have velvet drapes in the living room and a shiny satin coverlet in the bedroom. Whatever the surface, its texture will affect the way we see its color. Smooth surfaces reflect more light, and their color will appear brighter, while matte surfaces absorb the light and so appear darker. You can capitalize on this fact when you are choosing color combinations for your paint effects. A gloss and matte version paint of the same color will create a subtle contrast when used together, while paints that contrast in both color and texture will make the biggest impact. The Frosted Glass Vase on pages 174–77 is an example of how a subtle contrast can be achieved using glass frosting on a clear glass vase, while the Shimmery Glazed Wall on pages 150–53 gives a similar effect using wall paint.

Above: Shades of blue together with white suit a sunny bedroom and help to make it feel cool.
Right: Brightly painted walls of this colonial house in Mexico provide a vivid contrast to the natural wood and stone textures of the staircase.

INSPIRATION AND DESIGN

Now that you have a grasp of how colors work together, you can start to think about which patterns to use in your paint effects, how to arrange them, and which colors will work best and in what different combinations. But first of all, you need some inspiration.

Inspiration is all around you; find it in nature, by traveling to other countries, by looking at books and magazines—even by sneaking a look in other people's homes.

Nature offers us flower, fruit, and foliage shapes, trees, cloud formations, animal and fossil forms, shells and seaweed, the movement of water, and much more besides. When you go on your travels, pay special attention to the colors and motifs of handicrafts and textiles, the shape and color of buildings, the colors of spices in a street market, and the art that you see in the different places of worship that you visit.

Books and magazines provide another great source of inspiration. They not only show you places you will never visit, but they are a way of seeing what people are doing in homes all over the world. You may see a paint effect that you love so much that you simply want to copy it entirely, or you may see a beautiful object in someone's home that can be the starting point for your own design. Other people's color schemes can also be a very fruitful place to start.

To start you off, take photographs of things that inspire you or tear pictures out of magazines and pin them all to a "mood board." Some people like to collect pebbles, leaves, pieces of dress fabrics, and so on, and instead of pinning them to a mood board, they put them all together in a large shallow box or basket. Whichever method you choose, you will gradually see a pattern emerging from your collection that will point the way to your favorite style or color. Then you can use that information to inspire your stenciled, stamped, or freehand image.

Below left and right: A jet of water or the ripple effect of sand dunes can provide the inspiration for a simple paint effect motif or a whole-room scheme.

Motifs from history

If you are planning a period-style room and want a paint effect that is in keeping, you need to be aware of the fact that certain motifs—and colors (see page 29)—send out a "period" message. Thus Greek key designs, acanthus leaves, trophy motifs, bows, and swags all imply traditional, while loose swirls, geometric shapes, stylized flowers, leaves and shells, and any motif with a freehand "feel" tend to work better in a modern setting.

One way to research historical motifs is to contact museums and libraries. They can put you in touch with historical societies that specialize either in your particular locality or in certain architectural periods. Other great sources of reference are the many specialty motif publications and Web sites or, if you are able to find them, vintage books, magazines, and advertisements—again, your library can help, or try secondhand bookstores.

Alternatively, books and magazines on period interiors can offer the inspiration you need. It is not quite the same as going to the primary source of, say, an eighteenth-century pattern book, but they are much more accessible.

Scale and arrangement

Now you need to ask yourself the following sorts of questions: "Do I choose a large-scale pattern for a wall stamp or a small-scale one?" "Do I cover an entire surface with a stenciled pattern or just a small area, perhaps to make a frame or border?" "Do I decorate all the walls of my room, just one, or perhaps only an alcove or niche?" "Do I arrange my design randomly or symmetrically?"

Unfortunately, there are no clear-cut answers to these questions: it is all a matter of taste and a question of experience. However, if you are trying to emulate a certain decorating style, the principles of that style may give you the answers you are looking for. For example, a period style of decoration will most likely call for symmetry and formality— a paneled wall effect achieved by using stenciled borders, or a wall treatment based on regularly spaced stripes, like the Curling Scroll Wall on pages 76–79. In contrast, the irregularly placed bold stamp-print of the Funky Bathroom Wall on pages 80–85, is more in keeping with a contemporary room.

Remember, too, that the idea of highlighting a single wall with color or pattern is a relatively modern one—until the second half of the twentieth century, people were far more

Above: While you are on your travels, notice the impression a building makes—green-painted shutters, gray-stone walls, repeated motifs of arches and grids, and patterned ironwork.

likely to have used the same decorating effect on all four walls of a room, so do not apply, say, a stenciled pattern to just one wall of a room unless you want a modern feel, and, in that case, a modern motif will work better than, say, a fleur-de-lis design, or one based on swags and cherubs.

Design and color

Now you are ready to choose the colors for your paint effects. To do this you need to understand that every color has a psychological effect, often connected with its "temperature." For example, watery blues and greens are meditative and calming, while reds and yellows are invigorating. For the same reason, lime green and tangerine—both of which have yellow in them—are zesty, lively colors. Take care with greens, though. If the green is too strong, rather than having a calming effect, it can make you feel uncomfortable.

Then there are colors that carry certain cultural references. For instance, in the Chinese tradition, color was used symbolically in Buddhist art to represent the forces of

nature—green represented wood, red was fire, yellow was earth, white was metal, and black was water. In many countries of the West, purple is associated with royalty, white with purity and cleanliness—which is why it is often used in bathrooms—black with mourning, and red with socialism and revolution.

If you are following a period style, color combinations based on the palettes of the time (see opposite) will be your starting point. If not, you need some other guidelines. As we have seen, harmonizing colors work well together, but if a scheme is made up of nothing but harmonious colors, it can end up looking completely bland and boring. This is your chance to use your paint effects to inject some pizzazz.

For instance, stencil a couple of picture frames with a subtle peach on mid-blue design and paint a freehand flower in deep peach onto a pale blue cushion to invigorate a harmonious blue living room, or paint one wall a rich maroon and spatter-paint a pink lampshade with another shade of maroon in a pale pink bedroom. You will find that the contrast colors help the main colors be seen to best advantage. Go easy on the contrast—too much, and the eye simply won't know where to look first.

Above, left and right: The Far East provides another rich source of inspiration just waiting to be tapped. Chinese calligraphy in boldly contrasting colors and Buddhist art may well spark an idea in your mind.

However you decide to apply your painted motif, whether it is stenciled, stamped, or applied freehand, your choice of color combinations within the motif itself can make a huge difference to the final effect. For instance, a large-scale pattern worked in strongly contrasting colors—a rich chestnut brown chrysanthemum flower stenciled over a pale beige wall, for example—will appear more dominant than the same motif worked in a slightly darker shade of the wall color. The Toy Chest Thumbprint on pages 136–41 can be worked in a primary color on a white background for a younger child, or in the more subtle coloring I show for a slightly older child. The Checkered Stamped Floor shown on pages 62–65 takes center stage, but carry it out in shades of white and off-white for a look that would work well in the sanctuary of a bedroom with its en suite bathroom.

Historical color palettes

If you are using a paint effect in a period room, be aware of changing fashions. These were largely governed by the fact that, as paint technology advanced, so the available color palettes changed.

Thus in the baroque period, deep greens and blues, certain reds, and gold were fashionable; Gustavian style calls for chalky, pale colors, mainly white and off-white, gray, and pale green; Federal paint colors were limited: the most popular were yellow, ocher, or white; while the Shakers used stronger colors—sage green, rich blue, gray-blue, and oxblood. Technological advances during the empire period brought stronger, brighter paint colors, so this period is characterized by some unusual color combinations—yellow ocher with dark gray, gray with bright green, green with gold, and maroon with gray-green are just a few.

Below: Art deco facades in Miami Beach, Florida.

Moving into the twentieth century, the modernist palette is generally monotone, consisting largely of black, white, and gray. Art deco, on the other hand, injected color into people's lives. It brought mint-green, pink, champagne, apricot, and lilac into the mix, giving it an altogether more feminine feel.

Recently there has been a revival of interest in so-called "retro" styles—the brilliant yellows and reds, eggshell blue, olive green, and black and white of the 1950s, or psychedelic shocking pink, purple, scarlet, and orange alongside the black and brown of the 1960s.

Nowadays there is such a demand for historically accurate paint colors that many paint manufacturers produce their own historic paint ranges. You now have a completely pain-free way of getting your period colors right.

LOOK BEFORE YOU LEAP

So, you have decided on your design, its scale, and its arrangement. Now you have to firm up on the colors you will use, and, to help you in this, you need to do some serious thinking about what actually looks right in your space.

Swatch boards

One of the tricks of the trade is to create a swatch board. Swatch boards are very often used by interior decorators when they want to present ideas to their clients and show them how an entire scheme will look. You will find it especially useful if you are planning a whole-room scheme based around a paint effect.

Take a large sheet of hardboard and cover it with plain white paper or a sheet of wallpaper lining paper. Next, glue samples of your room's intended floor covering onto the board, together with samples or swatches of fabrics, trims, wallpapers, or tiles. If you wish, you can also include photographs of any furniture you already have or are intending to buy—tearing sheets from magazines or catalogs will do perfectly.

When it comes to adding your choice of paint colors, either cut out paint chips from the manufacturer's shade cards and glue them on, or paint pieces of card stock with the colors you are planning to use.

When you look at the overall effect of the board, you will be able to see how everything on it works together. Do the colors of the room scheme look a little bland? If so, do you need more tonal contrast (see page 24), or some color contrast accents (see page 28)? You might be able to introduce these as part of your paint effect, for example, by using a darker shade of paint for a stamp or stencil or by choosing a contrast color where you had thought that a toning shade would work. Would some different textures help, for instance nubbly cushions to contrast with a smooth leather sofa? Again, your paint effect can help you here— perhaps some shimmer-effect paint (see pages 150-53) or some scraffito work (see pages 158-61) will introduce the texture you need.

Opposite: Trying out colors on a white board before you start helps you to see if a color works well in different lights.

Testing, testing

Because colors vary in different lights, at different times of day, and in different seasons (see page 33), you should test out your colors carefully before you take the plunge and execute your paint effect for real.

As when making a swatch board, for testing paint colors you need to start either with some sheets of hardboard or some large card stock. If you are choosing a paint effect for a whole wall, then the bigger the surface you use for testing, the better. Color used on a small surface looks completely different than that used over a large expanse.

Now you need to know if your color requires a light or a dark undercoat. Generally speaking, a dark paint requires a dark—often gray—undercoat, while light colors are applied over white. The staff in your paint store can advise you.

Let us assume that you need a white undercoat. Paint the board white or use pure white card stock. Now paint your trial color all over the board or card stock and leave it to dry thoroughly. Once it has dried, pin or tape the board to a wall by the window and hold your mood board with its swatches nearby to check that the color works with the other colors in the room. Check it in the morning, at noon, and in the evening, then move the color sample to a darker area of the room and repeat the experiment. Finally, check the color sample in artificial light (see page 33).

If your main wall color is to be, say, blue, you could try painting three different blue sample boards—one in the blue you have your heart set on, one in a blue with a touch more gray, and one in a blue with a hint of red in it. That way you will see which shade of blue will work best in the differing light conditions.

You can even apply this testing technique to the whole paint effect, not just to the base color. Doing this also has the advantage of giving you a chance to practice the paint effect in a place where it does not matter if you make a mistake before you get down to the real thing.

citronella

sweet violet

minchester Red

canary

Fern Green

Happy violet

Sunflower 2589   Price Group B

Real Red 2085   Price Group B

Lime 2591   Price Group B

new

Above: This detailed swatch board for a retro-style room not only shows a wide range of possible paint colors, but it also includes fabric swatches and pictures of accessories—a table and chairs, some cups and saucers, and even some storage boxes. The next step might be to limit the paint colors to two main colors and a couple of contrasts. Alternatively, the board could become the basis for a whole-house retro-style scheme.

Say, for example, you are going to stencil your wall with the Curling Scroll Wall pattern (see pages 76–79). Follow the instructions given for the project but paint the background color and the stenciled design on your large sheet of card stock or board. We have used green-blue stenciled with white, but this may not suit your color scheme at all, in which case, try out some different color combinations.

Similarly, you may want to stencil a feather design onto your curtains as we did on pages 86–89. The shiny glazed navy-blue fabric and blue and white paints that we used may not be what you want. Again, try out different combinations—this simple design would look good in russet on a sheer white curtain, for example, or in pale blue on white. Once you have stenciled a sample length of fabric, pin it up near the window and view it in different lights. This time you do not have to move the sample to a different part of the room, as it will always be viewed near the window.

In the same way, if you want to test out a color combination for, say, the Checkered Stamped Floor (see pages 62–65), use the biggest piece of board or card stock you can for your trial, and when it is complete, lay it on the floor to view it in different lights.

One small tip: you do not have to buy a big can of paint to make your color sample boards. Most paint manufacturers now sell trial pots in a wide range of colors and paint finishes, so there is no excuse not to try before you buy.

Color and light

Not only can we only see color when there is light, but we see it differently according to the light source. Natural daylight shows colors at their truest, but that daylight will vary according to the season and time of day.

You can manipulate the effect of the light in a room according to the colors you use, for instance, choosing a warm color for a north-facing room that feels cold, and a cool color to soften the effect of strong sunlight in a room.

When choosing colors, you should consider a room's artificial light. Full-spectrum lights mimic daylight and give a clear, white light. Fiber-optic lights give a clean white light that can bleach colors, and halogen lights sometimes reduce the impact of strong colors. Tungsten bulbs give a soft, yellowish light that can make whites appear to be off-white. Candles give a flattering warm glow but can have a similar effect on color as tungsten light, while fluorescent lights do not flatter rich colors.

Top: A room filled with natural daylight.

Bottom: An artificially lit room.

TOOLS AND BRUSHES

A lot of the materials shown here are things you will already have around the house, especially if you already do your own painting and decorating. However, you need to check that you have a wide enough range of equipment for the paint effects projects you are aiming to do, and you may also need to go shopping in a specialty store for some of the products.

Brushes

You will need a good selection of brushes, both for painting large areas and for doing more detailed work. Generally speaking, the longer the bristles, the smoother the finished result will be. Firstly, you will need some large decorator's brushes for the walls and floors, a few medium-sized brushes for some of the "artwork" projects, fine and medium artist's brushes for doing fine work, and stenciling brushes for filling in stencils. Stenciling brushes come in a variety of types; most people prefer to work with those that have flexible bristles.

Rollers

A decorator's paint roller is useful for quickly covering large areas such as walls and floors. It can sometimes be used after brushing on paint to smooth out the brush marks. A small roller for applying paint to stamps can also be useful (see page 50).

Sponges

A selection of sponges in varying sizes and of different materials is essential. Cellulose sponges are useful for cleaning surfaces before painting them, but they can also be cut into stamps (see page 47), and can be used for applying paint (see pages 60–61 and 78). Sea sponges may also be used for applying paint, either to large areas, such as walls, or in conjunction with stencils (see pages 52, 96–97, 131, 144, and 165–66). The finished result will look more open than that achieved using a cellulose sponge.

Adhesives

A variety of adhesives are used to carry out the projects in this book. If you are attaching a backing board to a paint stamp (see pages 47 and 49), you will need a contact adhesive or general household adhesive. Repositionable stencil adhesive spray is a good choice for gluing a design to a sheet of card stock or stencil card prior to cutting out a stencil (see pages 51 and 72). Alternatively, you can use spray mount adhesive. You will also need a glue spreader or a piece of stiff cardboard.

Containers

You will need plenty of paint containers of varying sizes: paint cans are useful for holding large quantities of paint, such as latex paint, while old saucers, cups, and jars can be requisitioned for small quantities. A large plate or tile is useful when you are applying paint to a stamp with a roller.

Protection

Protect surfaces, your house, and yourself while you work. Drop cloths and plastic sheeting are essential. A decorator's mask will protect you from dust and fumes; masking tape in a variety of widths protects from paint smudges. Other must-haves include an old shirt or an apron to wear over your clothes, a supply of old newspaper, clean cloths, and kitchen towels.

Specialty equipment

The projects in this book are not difficult, but some specialty equipment is used. If you plan on developing your skills, you will certainly need a range of these. With some ingenuity, household items can be used to avoid any expensive outlay. For instance, if you don't own a potter's needle or awl, used for carrying out scraffito work for the Mexican-Style Flowerpots on pages 158–61, try using a knitting needle or other sharp object. For specialty equipment needed for making stencils and stamps (see pages 47–51), cast your mind back to your school days, and experiment with sponges, or even potatoes.

rollers

containers

masking tape

adhesive

UHU The All Purpose Adhesive

decorator's mask

potter's awl

brushes

STAINLESS

sponges

PAINTS AND VARNISHES

Paints are made of a pigment that provides the color, a binder, which makes the pigment stick to the surface beneath, and the vehicle—the liquid that dilutes the binder and makes it possible to apply the paint by brush. In the case of oil paints, the binder is a solvent that evaporates as the paint dries. Solvents are also used in water-based paints, but in far smaller quantities, which is why latex paint has far less odor than, say, eggshell paint. There is an enormous range of paints on the market. Here we look at those that are used for the projects in this book.

Primer

Wood and plaster surfaces that have not been painted before, or that have been rubbed or sanded back, are very absorbent. Unless you have primed them correctly, the paint you apply will simply sink right in, particularly with new plaster or drywall. The topcoat will determine the type of primer you use, so if, on new plaster, you are planning on a topcoat of latex paint, which is water-soluble, use diluted latex paint as a primer; if you want a topcoat of an oil-based paint, you will need to use a special stabilizing primer.

For priming wood trim, you can use a universal acrylic primer or special wood primer beneath your first coat. If you are working with MDF, chipboard, or hardboard, prime with latex paint or treat as wood.

If you are priming metal, there are specialty metal primers, some of which are available in spray cans.

Latex paint

We take this water-based paint for granted, but it did not really come into existence until the second half of the twentieth century when advances in the plastics industry made its development possible. Now it is the most commonly used paint for interior surfaces. Being low-odor, it is pleasant to use. It can also be readily washed out from brushes and rollers using just soap and water. It comes in a huge range of colors and a wide variety of finishes with different gloss levels, ranging from flat, through eggshell, satin, and semi-gloss, to high-gloss. All latex paints are washable but they vary in scrubbability. Flat paints have a very matte finish and are good for low-traffic areas such as bedrooms. Eggshell paints have a smooth finish and a

subtle sheen. They are scrubbable and suit bedrooms, hallways, and family rooms. Satin paints may be used in any room and are slightly more scrubbable than eggshell paints. Semi-gloss paints are even more durable. They are great for children's rooms and for any room where there is a lot of moisture, such as a bathroom. They are also very serviceable for painting trim. High-gloss paints are extremely reflective and are also the most scrubbable. Use them for highlighting trim and moldings, and for surfaces that receive a lot of wear, such as doors and cabinets.

Acrylic paint

Acrylic resins were first devised in Germany in 1901 and were manufactured commercially in the United States in the 1930s. Acrylic polymers were derived from the resins and proved superb as binders for pigments, with the result that today's relatively environmentally friendly acrylic artists' paints have an unparalleled brilliance and offer an enormous range of color possibilities. With their rather thick consistency, they adhere to almost any surface, can easily be thinned, and readily wash out of brushes using only water. They are also very durable and are available in gloss or matte finishes. Like latex paint, acrylic paints are useful as a base if you wish to mix your own colors.

Artist's oil paint

Sold in tubes and with a creamy consistency, traditional oil paints as used by artists come in a huge range of colors with good pigment strength. They are useful in paint techniques for coloring other oil-based paints or waxes. They do not wash out in water, though; you will need to use denatured alcohol.

Gilt cream

This is a soft wax compound that can be applied with the fingers or with a short-bristled brush such as a toothbrush. It comes in a range of different colors that includes several shades of gold, plus silver and pewter. If you are using it on its own, you can achieve variations in the color by applying successive layers, or by mixing one or more colors. It may be buffed up to a shine with a soft cloth or silk brush.

Metallic spray paint

This offers an alternative to gilt cream for achieving a metal look. Especially useful for items, such as the Verdigris Planters (see pages 162–67), that will be used outdoors. Like gilt cream, metallic spray paints come in a variety of different metal colors—golds, silver, copper, brass, and pewter, for example.

Fabric paint

This can be applied straight from the can to the fabric with a brush using freehand techniques, or it can be used in conjunction with stencils or stamps. When the paint is dry, it can be made permanent by fixing with an iron.

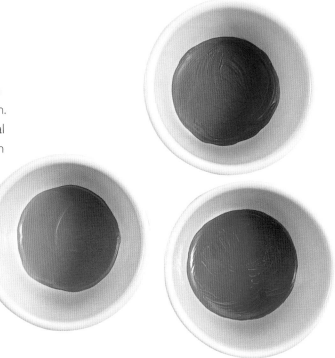

Following the manufacturer's instructions, cover the painted area with a clean cloth and, using the iron on the hottest setting, iron for one or two minutes. Fabric paint leaves the fabric soft, and the painted fabric can be washed as normal.

Heritage paints

Old-fashioned oil paints used a binder or resin derived from a natural vegetable oil such as linseed, usually dissolved in a solvent of turpentine. Modern oil paints use a synthetic type of resin called "alkyd," normally dissolved in mineral spirits. Whichever you are using, always work in a well-ventilated area to avoid inhaling the unpleasant-smelling and unhealthy fumes. Use denatured alcohol or a proprietary brush cleaner to clean brushes.

The forerunners of latex paint were limewash, distemper, and tempera. They are suspensions of powdered pigment in water, sometimes using egg as a binder. These were used for centuries on walls and ceilings, and produce an attractive dry, flat, chalky finish that many people think is more varied and more attractive—especially in period homes—than latex paint. It looks good as it ages, and since it does not contain plasticizers, it "breathes," allowing any damp in the wall to escape, which is another reason for its popularity in old homes. Distempers and temperas were unavailable for many years, but there has been a recent revival of interest in them and they are now produced in a wide range of colors.

Porcelain paint

This is a water-based product that comes ready-to-use in a bottle for freehand application or for use in conjunction with stamps or stencils. After firing in the oven, the treated objects are scratch-resistant and dishwasher-safe. There is a large range of excellent colors, with good depth and sheen, and because the paint is water-based, it can be thinned with water, though this will make the colors slightly more transparent. You can mix colors, too, if you wish, to achieve the color of your choice.

Porcelain paint also comes in tubes with an applicator nozzle for outlining or writing on china. These paints can be fixed in the oven in the same way.

Varnish

A finishing coat of varnish provides protection for your project from dents and nicks. You will probably want to use varnish on items such as furniture, picture frames, and flowerpots, and anything that needs to be durable.

Polyurethane varnishes are extremely durable but take a long time to dry and are harmful if inhaled. The usual choice nowadays, though slightly less durable, is nonyellowing acrylic varnish. This comes in gloss or matte finish and may be applied by brush or spray.

Crackle glaze

As they dry out over a long period of time, traditional oil-based paints and varnishes crack and craze. Recently people have sought to

reproduce this effect, and there are now a number of products on the market to help to achieve an instant "aged" look. Acrylic-based, the crackle glaze is applied over a coat of latex paint, left to dry, and then topped with a coat of latex paint in a different color. When the top coat dries, the crackle glaze does its work, causing the top coat to crack, revealing veins of the color beneath.

Glass frosting

Traditionally, hydrofluoric acid was the method employed to etch glass, by using a wax resist stencil to keep the acid off the parts of the glass that were not to be etched. Today you can achieve an etched or frosted-glass look with specialty acrylic-based frosting varnishes. These come as creamy liquid or spray-on versions.

Beeswax

This has been used for centuries to "feed," polish, and protect wooden surfaces, but it can also be mixed with pigments to produce colored wax for tinting wood. Although pretinted beeswax is available, it is much more fun—and not difficult—to blend your own color.

PREPARATION OF SURFACES

There is no point putting a lot of effort into your paint effect project if you have not prepared the surface properly. Without correct preparation, it will not be long before the paint cracks, lifts, or is rubbed off. Before you start, the surface must be clean, grease-free, smooth, free of cracks or holes, and correctly primed.

The different surfaces you will have to prepare if you are carrying out the projects in this book are walls, floors, furniture, fabrics, porcelain—including tiles—and metal.

Walls must be dusted and washed with a solution of mild detergent. Dishwashing liquid is perfectly adequate. If a wall has been papered, the paper is in good condition, and it is not torn or lifting at the edges, you can paint on top, but do a test patch first to be sure that the color of the paper does not "bleed" through. If the paper cannot be painted over, there is no alternative but to remove it completely, using a stripping knife with water and a little detergent, or with special stripping fluid. You could also use a steam stripper.

If there are cracks or holes in the wall, use a filling knife with a filler, then sand for a smooth finish.

Preparing wood

If you are painting on old floorboards, prepare the boards by hammering down any protruding nails, then vacuum and wash the floor to remove dirt and grease. You should prime bare boards with a wood primer (see page 36).

If the boards have already been painted or varnished, you will need to remove the old finish by sanding—mechanically or by hand—but be sure to do this after you have hammered down any nails, or the sandpaper or sanding belt will be torn as you work. Once you have finished sanding, prepare the floor for painting with a primer.

New wood, whether on a floor or in furniture, only needs a light sanding to provide a "tooth" or surface for the paint to adhere to.

Old furniture, and old painted or varnished floorboards, must have old, flaking paint or varnish removed. If the finish is in reasonable condition, rub it down with steel wool dipped in denatured alcohol, then leave it to dry. If the finish is very bad, remove it completely using a paint or varnish stripper. Fill any holes or gouges using a wood filler.

Preparing fabric

Fabric must be washed and dried to remove the "sizing" before you apply fabric paint. It must then be ironed. If the fabric is to be made up into, say, a curtain or a tablecloth, it is best to hem it after washing and ironing, and before you apply the paint.

Preparing porcelain

China and tiles must be completely clean and grease-free before you apply paint. Remove any grease with denatured alcohol, then wash with detergent and dry thoroughly.

Preparing metal

Metal also needs to be completely clean and grease-free. Remove any grease with denatured alcohol and, if the metal is old and rusting, rub it down with steel wool to remove any rust flakes.

You will need . . .

- Rubber gloves to protect your hands. If you are allergic to latex, use special nonallergic latex gloves.
- Feather duster for dusting over walls before you paint.
- Sponge for washing surfaces.
- Stripping knife for removing old wallpaper.
- Filler and filling knife for filling cracks in walls or wood.
- Sandpaper in various grades.
- Electric sander with shaped heads and attachments to make sanding easier.
- Hammer for nailing down old floorboards.
- Steel wool for removing old paint or varnish from furniture.
- Denatured alcohol and lighter fluid for removing grease from china, glass, and furniture.

MEASURING AND MARKING

There is no getting away from it. Carrying out the projects in this book will require some careful measuring and marking. If you fail to do this, you will spoil the look of the finished paint effect, and you may even find, as you work, that, horror of horrors, your design is too big or too small to fit the allocated space.

If you are planning a repeating design across a floor or wall, you need to measure the dimensions of the surface and plan the size of your pattern so it fits perfectly into the space. For example, you may want to use the Curling Scroll Wall design on pages 76–79. What a pity it would be if you found that the last row of motifs across the wall did not fit completely. It is far better to measure the height and width of the wall and plan the spacing between the vertical rows of the design, as well as the appropriate width of the motif itself, so it fits perfectly.

The same applies if you are planning to paint a border on a floor or wall. Be sure to measure the distance of the border from the edge and mark it lightly to guide you as you paint.

When it comes to using a stencil in the center of a panel or door, check that you have positioned the motif in the true center of the stencil and that you hold the stencil with its edges equidistant from the edges of the door or panel. When using a stamp, mark the center point of the surface to be stamped before stamping on the mark.

Plumb line and level

A level is used for horizontal or vertical lines. You can attach a small level to a length of timber to help you mark vertical or horizontal lines on a wall surface.

A plumb line ensures that upright lines, for example, down a wall, are truly vertical. It is named after the Latin word for lead (*plumbum*) that would have weighted the end of the string. Coat the string with soft chalk, either powdered French chalk or blackboard chalk along the length. Hang the plumb line from the top of the wall with a thumbtack, allowing gravity to pull the weight to the bottom in a straight line. Hold the base of the string firmly and snap the string against the wall to mark your vertical line. Some lines come with an automatic chalking facility, although French chalk has a number of other useful applications.

Graph paper

Use this to plan out a design across a wall or floor. A scale of 1:10 is good if you are using metric measurements, otherwise a scale of 1:12 is best.

Tracing papers

These offer a means of transferring a template or design to the surface being painted. Graphite paper is an alternative to ordinary tracing paper and works much like old-fashioned carbon paper, while for fabrics you can buy special fabric transfer paper.

Pencils, pens, and eraser

You will use these a lot, both for planning out your designs and for marking surfaces. If you use a soft pencil to mark a wall, for example, you will be able to erase any marks that still show after you have finished painting.

If you are uncertain about your freehand painting skills, use a china marker or wax pencil to mark your design on ceramic or shiny surfaces. The marks can be rubbed off easily when you have finished.

Marker pens are useful for drawing the outline of a template onto sponge to make a stamp, or onto stencil card to make a stencil.

String and thumbtacks

These are invaluable for drawing arcs or circles of different sizes (see page 134) and to stand in for a plumb line.

Rulers

You cannot have too many of these. A retractable steel tape measure is vital for measuring distances over walls and floors. A plastic and a steel ruler will be useful in the planning stages, when you are designing your motif and enlarging a template to the correct size.

graph paper

tracing papers

retractable steel tape measure

string

thumbtacks

chalk

plumb line

level

rulers

eraser

pencils

scissors

marker pens

TECHNIQUES
AND PROJECTS

STAMPING AND STENCILING

Stamping and stenciling are techniques that have been used for centuries to decorate walls, floors, fabrics, furniture, and household objects. Because they are so easy to adapt to suit any style of decorating project, they have never really gone out of fashion. Choose from one of the huge range of ready-made stencils or stamps, or let your imagination fly, and design and make your own.

Materials for stamps

❶ Stamping is quicker than stenciling and suits small, simple motifs best. You can cut your stamps from foam rubber or sponge in various thicknesses—neoprene foam or the sort of foam that is used for yoga mats or camping sleeping mats works well. You can also use a cellulose bath sponge, but it will give a rougher looking result. Another alternative is to use one of the many ready-made stamps in a variety of styles that are on the market.

❷ If you are using one of the thinner sorts of foam, it is best to glue several layers together and to attach the stamp to a backing board made of a piece of cardboard, wood, or plywood. Use contact adhesive to do this. The finished stamp will be easier to grip, and it will be easier to apply weight evenly as you work.

❸ You can even cut a small stamp from an eraser. This is easy to hold, so it will not need a backing board.

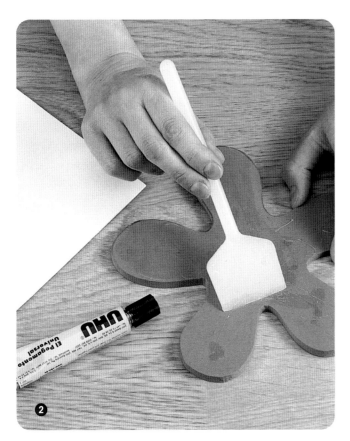

Making a stamp

① If you are using a template to make a stamp, trace the template onto tracing paper. Enlarge the tracing to the required size on a photocopier or using the grid technique on page 108.

② Then simply hold the template in position on the foam and draw around it using a pencil. Bear in mind that when you use the stamp, you will be applying a mirror image to the surface you are working on. Often this does not make much difference to the end result, but if it does—for example, if you plan on stamping numbers or letters— remember to turn the template over before you mark the cutting line or you will end up stamping gobbledygook!

③ Working on a cutting mat, use a craft knife to cut carefully around the marked outline. If you are gluing several layers of foam together to make a stamp (see previous page), glue them after you mark the outline but before you cut out the stamp. If necessary, once you have cut the stamp, glue it to the backing board.

Making a stamp from string

You can also use string to make your stamp. This especially suits designs based on circles and spirals.

① Draw your deign on a piece of stiff card stock and apply household glue from a tube with a nozzle over the pencil lines.

② Press the string into the adhesive and leave to dry.

③ Your stamp is then ready to use.

Tip
● The piece of card stock works well as a backing here, because the stamp is applied to a curved lampshade and the card stock is slightly flexible.

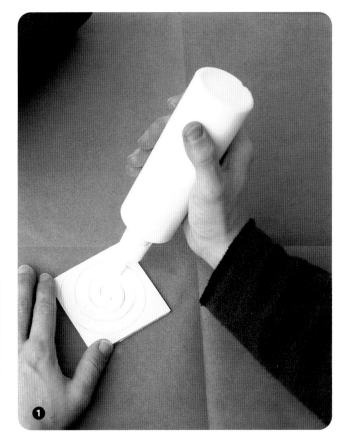

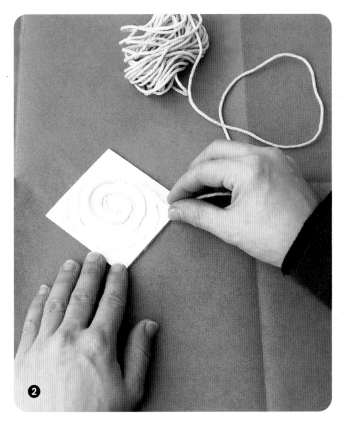

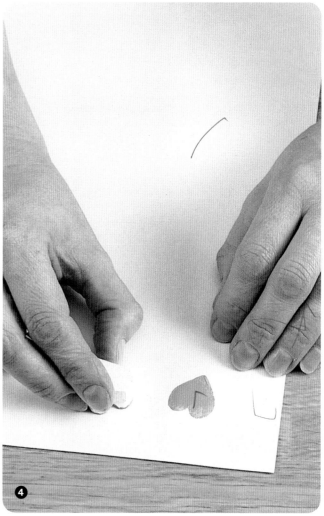

Applying the paint to the stamp

1 To achieve a smooth result when you stamp, apply the paint to the stamp using a small roller.

2 If the stamp is very small, spread the paint onto a dish or tile using a brush or roller, then press the stamp into the paint to load it up.

3 An alternative method of loading the stamp with paint is to simply to paint it on the stamp with a small brush. This will give a slightly rougher finish to the print.

4 Always reload the stamp with paint for each print and try it out before you start to make sure that you are applying pressure evenly.

Materials for stencils

Stencils can be far more complex than stamps, and some are difficult to design, but those used in this book are all very straightforward. You can cut a stencil from paper, card stock, plastic, or clear acetate. The plastic and acetate are the most durable and are best if you have to use the stencil repeatedly. This will avoid the stencil falling to pieces halfway through the project! Clear acetate is an especially useful material, as you can see through it to mark and cut your stencil. It is also easier to position during use.

Making a stencil

❶ If you are using a template to make a stencil, there are various ways of getting the motif onto the stencil material. One is to enlarge the template to the required size on a photocopier, then use repositionable stencil spray adhesive or spray mount adhesive to attach the photocopy to the stencil material.

❷ Working on a cutting mat, use a craft knife to cut through both the photocopy and the stencil material. Be bold as you cut so the cut is as clean as possible. Any irregularities will spoil the outline of the stenciled design.

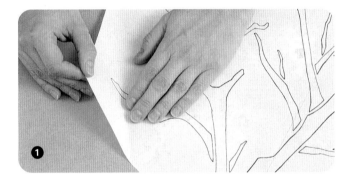

❸ Alternatively, if you are using acetate to make the stencil, you can hold the acetate over a photocopied or drawn design, secure it on a cutting mat with masking tape, and cut the stencil out.

Tip
● If you are going to stencil a large area such as a wall, cut extra stencils before you begin. That way, if a stencil gets damaged, you can discard it and carry on working without holding up your work.

Using a stencil

1 Make sure that the stencil is held securely in place as you work. The most common way of achieving this is to fix it to the surface using masking tape. An alternative is to use special stencil mount spray.

2 Pour a little paint into a dish and dip the tip of the stenciling brush into the paint.

3 Blot off any excess paint on paper towels or a clean cloth. The brush should be almost dry; otherwise, paint will seep under the edges of the stencil.

4 Hold the brush perpendicular to the surface and apply the paint from the edges of the stencil toward the center, using a dabbing motion.

5 You can also apply the paint using a sponge. Again, use only a little paint on the sponge and remove any excess before you start.

6 Remove the stencil carefully when you have finished to prevent smearing and to be sure that the masking tape does not damage the surface.

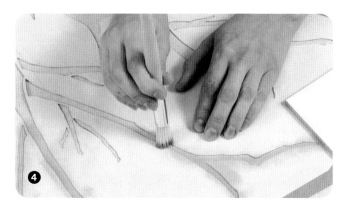

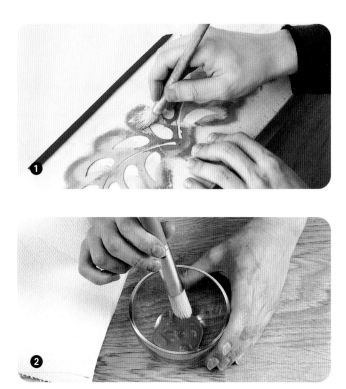

Shading effects

A shading effect adds a delightful touch to a stencil and is easily achieved. When you have finished stenciling with the first color, simply apply a little of a second color carefully to the edges of the stencil.

Stamping with stenciling

Combining stenciling with stamping opens up fresh new possibilities. It enables you to add a second—or even a third—color to your design as well as more detail to a simple stamped image.

❶ First apply the stamp, then leave the paint to dry.

❷ Position the stencil on top of the stamped image and work the stencil in a second color.

Fern stenciled floor

This stenciled pattern on floorboards is inspired by the skeletal leaf forms that were popular in the 1950s and were used by the likes of textile designer Lucienne Day. The coloring is distinctly retro, too— this moss green was a favorite.

YOU WILL NEED:

- graph paper
- 2-in. paintbrush
- ¼ gal. wood primer
- ½ gal. white satin
  or eggshell latex paint
- soft pencil
- tracing paper
- paper
- stencil plastic
- cutting mat
- masking tape
- craft knife
- size 8 artist's brush
- 10 fl. oz. moss green
  satin or eggshell latex paint
- ¼ gal. clear matte varnish

These quantities are for a floor
measuring 180 square feet.

1 Plan your design on graph paper, bearing in mind where any large pieces of furniture will be placed. Prepare the floorboards as described on page 40, prime with wood primer, then paint with two coats of white satin or eggshell latex paint using the 2-in. brush.

2 If you wish, lightly mark the positions of the leaves on the floorboards using a soft pencil. Trace the leaf template on page 182 onto paper and enlarge to the required size. Place the stencil plastic over the enlarged template and secure on a cutting mat with masking tape. Using a craft knife, carefully cut out the stencil.

3 Following your planned design, secure the stencil to the floor using masking tape.

4 Using the size 8 artist's brush, apply the moss green paint to the stencil. Carefully remove the stencil, clean any paint from the underside, and reposition it where necessary. Leave the floor to dry, then varnish with clear matte varnish.

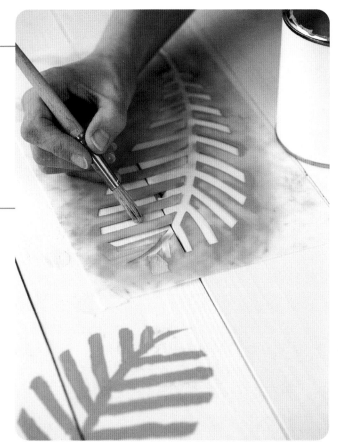

Tip

• Using an artist's brush to apply the paint gives a smooth finish. If you want a stippled effect, use a stencil brush.
• If you would like to make the floor resemble a painted floorcloth, paint a border—perhaps a broad line with a narrower line inside—around the edges of the floor.

Leaf-stamped limed floor

This project is ideal for a den or sunroom overlooking the garden, or for any room where bare floorboards are more practical than carpet. The design capitalizes on the contrast between the glossy stamped leaves and the matte limed-effect allover wash.

1

Prepare the floorboards as described on page 40. "Age" new floorboards like these with a base coat wash made from one part blue-gray satin or eggshell latex paint mixed with three parts mineral spirits. Apply the wash using a sponge and broad, sweeping movements. Leave to dry thoroughly.

YOU WILL NEED:

- paint container
- ¼ gal. blue-gray satin or eggshell latex paint
- 1¾ gal. mineral spirits
- 2 household sponges
- tracing paper
- thick foam rubber
- chalk or pencil
- cutting mat
- craft knife
- cardboard or tile
- small roller
- ¼ gal. polyurethane gloss varnish
- ruler
- 2-in. paintbrush
- ¼ gal. lime-white satin or eggshell latex paint

These quantities are for a floor measuring 180 square feet.

2

Use the two small leaf templates (page 183) to make the stamps from the foam rubber, following the directions on page 48. If your floor area is very large, you may want to enlarge the templates. Pour a little gloss varnish onto a flat surface such as an old tile or piece of cardboard. Pick up a small amount of varnish on the roller and apply an even coat to a leaf stamp.

3 Apply the two leaf stamps alternately around the edge of the room, 6 in. away from the baseboard. Change the angle of the stamps to give a more varied effect. Leave to dry thoroughly, then apply a wash of one part lime-white satin or eggshell latex paint and four parts mineral spirits. Brush on evenly in the direction of the grain.

4 Once the wash has begun to soak into the wood, wipe over the stamps with a clean sponge or cloth. The leaf shapes will become visible as the wash dries.

Checkered stamped floor

Pastel shades of creamy yellow, lilac, and mauve bring a springlike look to a room and give a fresh new twist to the traditional checkered floor. This design is not difficult, but be sure to measure the dimensions of your room carefully before you cut your stamps so that the design fits as perfectly as possible. Forward planning is essential.

YOU WILL NEED:

- graph paper
- pencil
- 1 sheet neoprene foam, 12 x 10 in.
- ruler
- craft knife
- cutting mat
- 2-in. paintbrush
- ¼ gal. wood primer
- 1-in. paintbrush
- ½ gal. pale gray-mauve satin or eggshell latex paint
- ¼ gal. cream satin or eggshell latex paint
- ¼ gal. pale yellow satin or eggshell latex paint
- ¼ gal. lilac satin or eggshell latex paint
- ¼ gal. mauve satin or eggshell latex paint
- ¼ gal. clear matte varnish

These quantities are for a floor measuring 180 square feet.

1 Plan your design on graph paper and cut two square neoprene foam stamps, one with its sides half as long as those of the other. We used 4 x 4-in. and 8 x 8-in. stamps, but you may find these sizes do not fit your floor. Prepare the floorboards as described on page 40, prime with wood primer, then apply two coats of pale gray-mauve satin or eggshell latex paint. Using the 1-in. brush, dab some cream and pale yellow paint onto the larger stamp. Do not blend the colors too much. Apply the stamp along one edge of the floor, leaving a gap equal to the length of one side of the stamp between each square. Once you have completed the first row, use those squares as a positioning guide for subsequent rows. Reload the stamp with the cream and pale yellow paint between each impression.

2 Take care as you remove the stamp to ensure that you do not smudge the paint. When the floor has been covered with the large squares, leave it to dry thoroughly.

3 Dab the lilac and mauve paints onto the smaller square stamp. Again, do not blend the colors too much. Position the smaller stamp over the intersection of the larger squares and stamp. Repeat until all the smaller squares have been stamped. Leave the floor to dry then varnish with clear matte varnish.

Stenciled numbers

This border design brings some color to plain white walls and will give any room a quirky touch. Plan the height of the border carefully—it works well about two-thirds of the way up the wall from the baseboard. If you position the numbers too low, chances are that they will simply be concealed by furniture.

1 Prepare the wall as described on page 40. If necessary, apply white latex paint to cover and leave to dry thoroughly. Using the templates on page 184, cut the number stencils and enlarge if required. Position the level at the desired height along the wall to ensure a straight line.

YOU WILL NEED:

- white latex paint (optional)
- tracing paper
- pencil
- stencil card
- craft knife
- cutting mat
- level
- ruler or tape measure
- stencil brush
- 2 fl. oz. olive green flat latex paint
- 2 fl. oz. mustard yellow flat latex paint
- 2 fl. oz. red flat latex paint
- cloth
- eraser

These quantities are for a wall measuring 108 square feet.

2 Draw a faint line in pencil along the top of the level to act as a guide for positioning the stencils.

3 Position the first stencil on the marked line. Holding it steady, use a gentle stippling motion with the stencil brush to dab the paint onto the stencil. Remove the stencil carefully and wipe any paint from its reverse using a damp cloth. Continue along the wall, spacing the stencils evenly and using the numbers and paint colors in a random order.

4 When all the paint is completely dry, carefully erase the pencil line.

Tip
● You could make your own stencils from stiff cardboard cut into small circles, squares, or other simple shapes.
● If you want a color scheme for a nursery, primary red, yellow, and blue are good choices. Try more sophisticated colors for elsewhere.

Shadowy tree room divider

What better way to bring the outdoors in than with this delicate stenciled tree? The shaded effect is simply achieved by stenciling with a second color along the edges of the stencil. Use the finished shade at a window, or be bold and hang it from the ceiling for a stylish room divider that would grace any boudoir. Whichever you choose, the result is sure to be stunning.

YOU WILL NEED:

- white fabric roller shade
- stencil board
- masking tape
- paper
- repositionable stencil adhesive spray or spray mount adhesive
- cutting mat
- craft knife
- 2½ fl. oz. pale gray flat latex paint
- ceramic tile or old plate
- ½-in. flat brush
- medium stencil brush
- 2½ fl. oz. mid-gray flat latex paint

These quantities are for a roller shade measuring 3 feet wide.

1 If the stencil board is not large enough to fit your shade, join two sheets of board edge to edge with masking tape. Apply the tape on both sides of the joint.

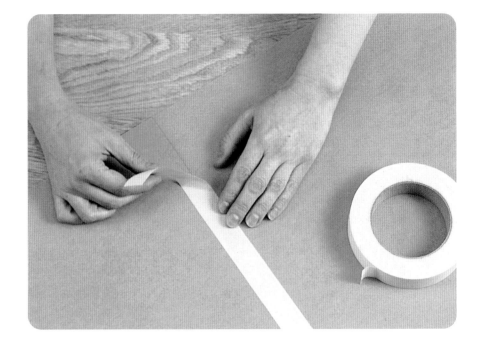

2 Enlarge the tree template (page 185) to fit your shade. Cut it out roughly then attach it to the stencil board with repositionable stencil adhesive spray or spray mount adhesive, smoothing the template from the center outward.

3 Resting on a cutting mat, cut out the stencil with a craft knife.

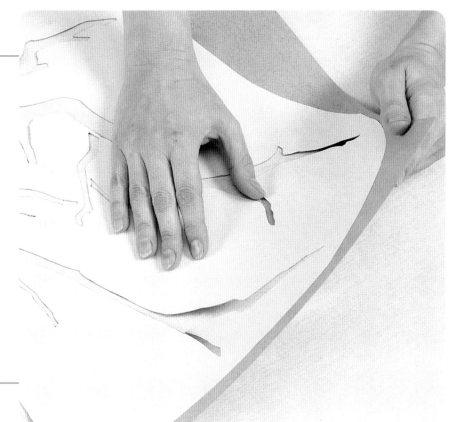

4 Mark the center of the blind, then spray the wrong side of the stencil with repositionable stencil adhesive spray and center it on the blind.

5 Apply a thin coat of pale gray flat latex paint to a ceramic tile or an old plate with a ½-in. flat brush.

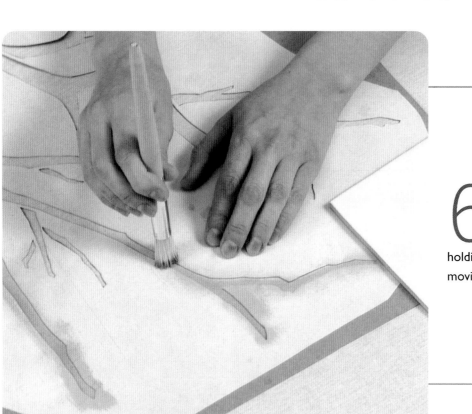

6 Dab at the paint with a stencil brush and stencil through the cutouts, holding the brush upright and moving it in a circular motion.

7 Apply a thin coat of mid-gray flat latex paint to a ceramic tile or an old plate with the flat brush. Dab at the paint with the stencil brush and stencil the edges of the tree to shade it. Remove the stencil.

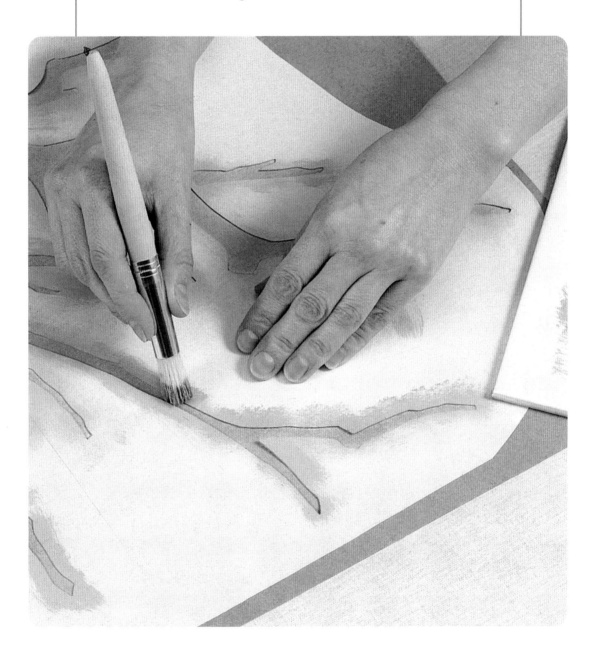

Curling scroll wall

The symmetry of a repeating curling scroll combined with a restrained color scheme creates an atmosphere of peace and tranquility that acts as the perfect foil to a classically furnished room. If you prefer a more modern look, the design will look equally effective in brown on beige or lilac on pale mustard-yellow or green.

YOU WILL NEED:

- graph paper
- pencil
- tape measure
- household sponge
- ½ qt. green-blue flat latex paint
- level
- length of wood the height of the wall between the baseboard and crown molding
- tracing paper
- clear acetate
- craft knife
- cutting mat
- masking tape
- stencil brush
- 4 fl. oz. white flat latex paint
- cloth or paper towels

These quantities are for a wall measuring 108 square feet.

1 Plan your design on graph paper to ensure that you can fit the spirals evenly across the wall. In this example, the lines of spirals are 12 in. apart. Prepare the wall as described on page 40. Dip one side of the sponge into the green-blue flat latex paint. Wipe off the excess on the side of the can. Use the sponge in a circular motion to apply the paint to the wall. This will give a soft mottled effect. If there are any bare patches once the paint is dry, dab on a little more paint. Leave to dry throughly.

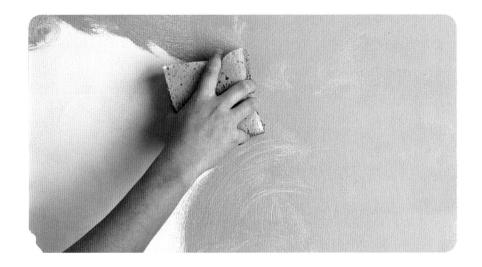

2 Working across the wall from left to right, mark points 12 in. apart. Tape a level to the length of wood with masking tape and use it to draw a vertical line through every marked point as a guide.

3 Using the template on page 186 and following the instructions on page 51, cut out the stencil, enlarging it as necessary. Place the stencil at the top of the wall, centering it over the first marked line and holding it in place at top and bottom with the masking tape. Dip the stencil brush into the white paint and wipe off any excess onto a cloth or paper towel. Apply the paint to the wall with the stencil brush, using a stippling motion.

4 Peel the stencil away from the wall from the bottom upward to prevent any smearing. Clean any paint from the reverse of the stencil, then reposition the stencil lower down the marked line to continue the design.

Funky bathroom wall

You won't be able to keep your eyes half-closed for long in the morning when you walk in your bathroom and see this funky design on the wall—it is sure to bring a smile to your face. The trick here is careful planning—work around your bathroom fixtures, and you will achieve truly professional results.

YOU WILL NEED:

- graph paper, tracing paper, soft pencil, eraser
- 4-in. paintbrush
- ¼ gal. white semi-gloss latex paint
- 5 fl. oz. lavender-blue semi-gloss latex paint
- ¾-in., 1-in. and 1½-in. flat brushes
- 2½ fl. oz. each deep red, pink, and jade green semi-gloss latex paint
- 3 sheets neoprene foam, each 12 x 10 in.
- all-purpose household glue
- glue spreader
- cutting mat and craft knife
- 8 x 8-in. mounting board
- ceramic tile or old plate
- medium round brush
- paper towels

These quantities are for a wall measuring 108 square feet.

1 Plot your design to scale on a sheet of graph paper before you begin.

2 Using the 4-in. brush, paint the wall with the white paint and leave to dry. Refer to the flower template (page 185), and use a soft pencil to draw a large flower head on the wall following your design. Draw lightly so that if you are not happy with your drawing you can erase it and start again.

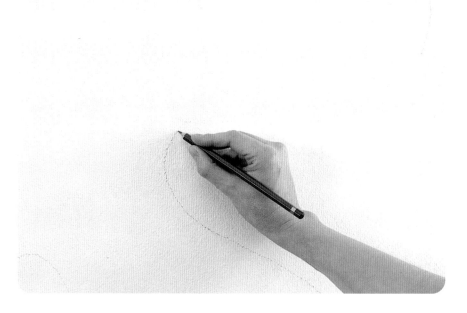

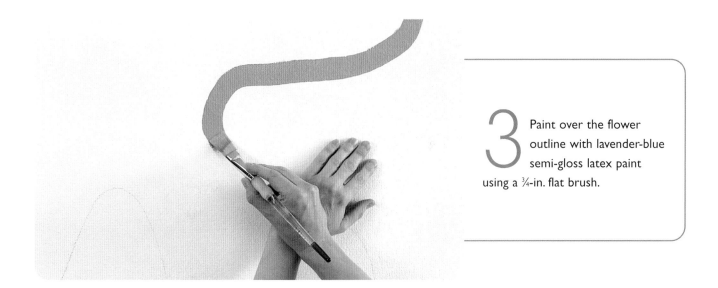

3 Paint over the flower outline with lavender-blue semi-gloss latex paint using a ¾-in. flat brush.

4 Fill in the flower with a 1½-in. brush and the same paint.

5 Leave the paint to dry. Using a 1-in. flat brush, paint an oval center on the flower using the deep red semi-gloss latex paint.

6 Cut three 8-in. squares of neoprene foam. Trace the flower template onto tracing paper, enlarge it if necessary on a photocopier or using the grid method (page 108), and cut it out. Draw around the template on top of one of the foam squares. Stick the squares together in layers with all-purpose household glue, with the flower square on top, using a plastic glue spreader or scrap of cardboard to spread the glue. Set the squares aside while the glue dries.

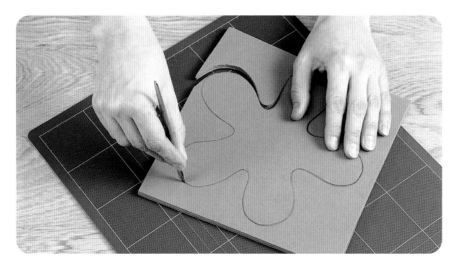

7 Resting on a cutting mat, hold a craft knife upright to cut out the flower. Center the flower on an 8 x 8-in. piece of mounting board.

8 Apply a coat of pink semi-gloss latex paint to a ceramic tile or old plate with a ¾-in. flat brush. Use a small roller to pick up the paint. Roll the paint onto the flower stamp.

9 Press the stamp firmly onto the wall, according to your design. Apply even pressure, then lift the stamp off the wall.

10 Use a medium round brush to fill in any gappy spots in the stamped flower.

11 Repeat to apply more flowers to the wall in pink, lavender-blue, deep red, and jade green semi-gloss latex paint, cleaning off the previous color paint from the stamp before it dries with moistened paper towels.

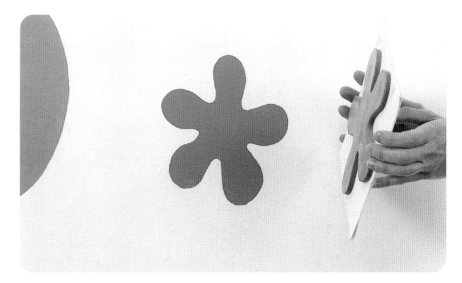

Feather curtain

The crisp combination of blue and white used for these curtains makes a striking statement that belies their simplicity. The trick here is not to overload the fabric with pattern repeats. Exercise some restraint as you position the stencil and you will achieve this calm, floating-feather look.

YOU WILL NEED:

- tracing paper
- pencil
- clear acetate
- craft knife
- cutting mat
- masking tape
- one pair navy blue curtains, store-bought or homemade
- fine dressmaker's pins or tailor's chalk
- cardboard
- medium stencil brush
- 5 fl. oz. white fabric paint
- paper towels or cloth
- 1 fl. oz. pale blue fabric paint

These quantities are for a pair of curtains measuring 48 in. wide and 63 in. long.

1 Using the template on page 183 and, enlarging it if necessary, cut the feather stencil from clear acetate. Whether you are using store-bought or homemade curtains, wash and iron them to remove any sizing and preshrink them. Lay each curtain flat on the floor or on a large worktable and plot the position of each feather. You can mark them with fine dressmaker's pins or tailor's chalk. Smooth one curtain out on a tabletop, and place a piece of cardboard under the fabric.

2 Hold the edge of the fabric in place using strips of masking tape.

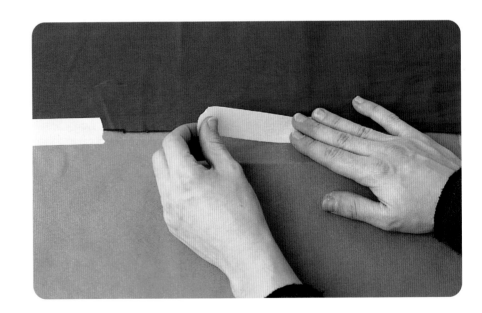

3 Position the stencil and hold it in place using more masking tape. Load the stencil brush with white fabric paint, taking care to remove any excess paint with paper towels or a clean cloth. Stipple the paint carefully over the stencil.

4 Using a clean brush and pale blue fabric paint, apply paint to the tips of the feather. Leave to dry thoroughly, then remove the stencil. Clean any paint from the reverse of the stencil, then repeat, moving the stencil to its new position. Always place a piece of cardboard beneath the area you are working on.

Gilded picture frames

Finding the right picture frame can be a thankless—and costly—task. This design, reminiscent of seventeenth-century picture frames with its drop shadow effect, will grace any classically furnished home. All you need to start is a pair of store-bought frames with some classical molding, and a broad, flat area to work on.

YOU WILL NEED:

- two wooden picture frames
- tracing paper
- pencil
- clear acetate
- cutting mat
- craft knife
- masking tape
- ½-in. flat artist's brush
- 9 fl. oz. black satin latex paint
- small stencil brush
- paper towels or a cloth
- gold gilt cream
- 1 fl. oz. gold acrylic paint

These quantities are for a pair of picture frames each measuring 14 x 12 in.

1 Using the template on page 186 and, enlarging it if necessary, cut the picture frame stencil from clear acetate. Using the flat artist's brush, paint the frames with black satin latex paint as a base coat. Leave to dry. Use a stencil brush to smooth a little gold gilt cream over the base coat, to give a metallic sheen.

2 Use masking tape to hold the stencil in position on the frame, and use a clean stencil brush to stipple on the black satin latex paint. Remove any excess paint from the brush with paper towels or a cloth before you begin to stencil. Leave the paint to dry.

3 Clean the stencil, then reposition it in order to leave a black line or shadow along one edge of the stenciled motif. With a clean stencil brush, stipple again, using gold acrylic paint. Leave to dry.

4 Remove the stencil carefully, and clean it before using it again. Reposition it on the picture frame to continue the pattern, then repeat the black and gold stippling. Continue the pattern to complete the frame, then repeat on the second frame.

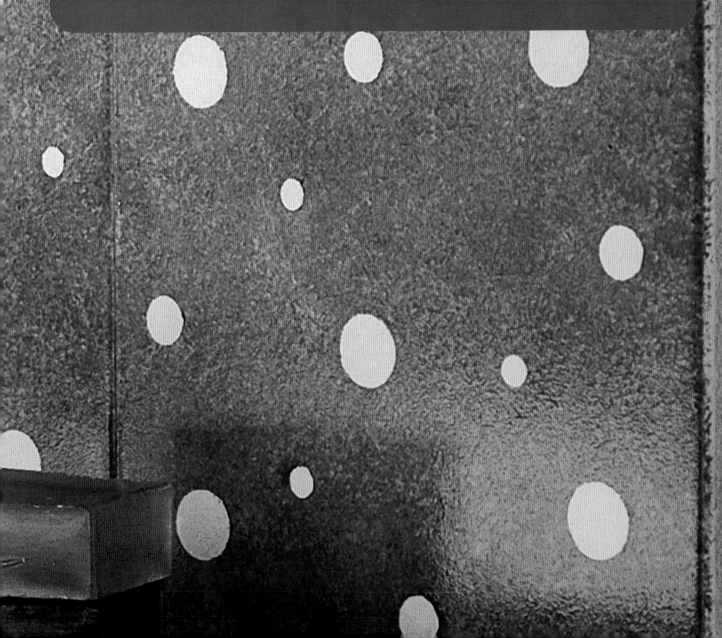

Bathroom backsplash

Extend your skills by using specialty porcelain paint, and make a splash in your bathroom at the same time. The combination of sponging and reverse stenciling on readily available self-adhesive stickers works like a charm. Bake the tiles in your oven when you have finished, and, before you know it, you'll have a brand-new look for plain white tiles.

YOU WILL NEED:

- a sheet of plastic or old plastic bags
- six square white tiles
- round paper stickers in assorted sizes
- ½-inch flat brush
- ceramic tile or old plate
- 1½ fl. oz. aquamarine porcelain paint
- sea sponge
- 1½ fl. oz. turquoise porcelain paint
- tile adhesive
- tile grout

These quantities are for six tiles, each measuring 8 x 8 in.

1 Lay a sheet of plastic or a layer of old plastic bags out flat to protect your work surface. Arrange the tiles in two rows of three, edge to edge on top of the plastic. Stick the largest paper stickers to the tiles in a curving diagonal band. Apply the remaining stickers around the band at random to fill any empty spaces.

2 Apply a coat of aquamarine porcelain paint to a ceramic tile or an old plate with a flat brush. Moisten a sea sponge and dab at the paint. Dab the paint onto the tiles to the right of the diagonal band.

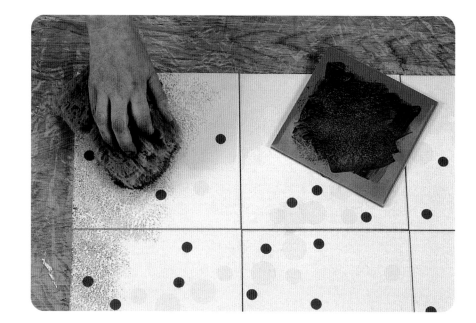

3 Repeat using turquoise paint on the other side of the band, merging the shades together along the band. Leave to dry and apply a second coat to deepen the color.

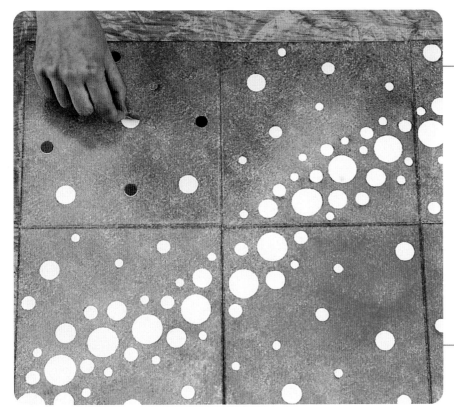

4 Leave the tiles to dry, then carefully peel off the stickers to reveal unpainted circles. Following the paint manufacturer's instructions, bake the tiles in an oven to set the paint. Stick the tiles to the wall above the sink using tile adhesive, and finish with white grout.

Pencil floorcloth

Need something to liven up a boring floor? Then look no further. This fabulous floorcloth can be yours in a matter of hours. Its graphic gray, black, and white design will suit a home study to perfection. The instructions won't trip you up, but to make sure the floorcloth doesn't either, use some special double-sided rug tape underneath.

YOU WILL NEED:

- thick calico or artist's canvas
- double-sided carpet tape
- plastic sheeting or plastic bags
- 3-in. paintbrush
- 15 fl. oz. white acrylic primer
- 15 fl. oz. white flat latex paint
- ½-in. masking tape
- card stock
- cutting mat and craft knife
- metal ruler
- size 4 flat artist's brush
- 2½ fl. oz. each of 4 shades of gray acrylic paint
- ceramic tile or old plate
- stencil brush
- piece of cardboard
- 2½ fl. oz. white acrylic paint
- 2½ fl. oz. black acrylic paint
- 1 qt. clear water-based varnish

These quantities are for a canvas measuring 50¾ x 37½ in.

1 To hem the floorcloth, press under 2 in. on the raw edges. Open out the corners and press diagonally across the raw edges. Cut away the excess at the corners ⅝ in. from the pressed corners. Stick the hems in place with double-sided carpet tape. You should end up with a floorcloth that measures 46¾ x 33½ in.

2 Press the cloth and lay it out flat on a sheet of plastic or plastic bags that have been cut open and laid flat. Use a 3-in. paintbrush to paint the floorcloth all over with white acrylic primer. Leave to dry, then apply a coat of white flat latex paint. Leave to dry again.

3 Run a line of ½-in. masking tape 1½ in. from both short edges and one long edge of the floorcloth.

4 Referring to the image of the completed floorcloth on pages 98–99, apply the masking tape in rows parallel with the short edges to make the pencils. Make five 3¼-in. wide pencils, four 2½-in. wide pencils, and five 2-in. wide pencils, alternating the widths.

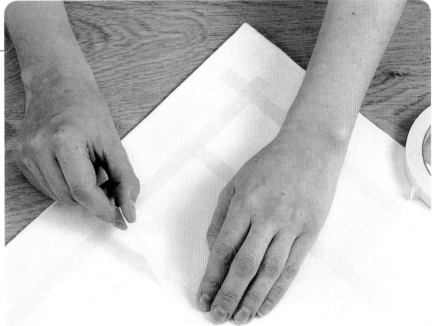

5 Trace the pencil point templates (page 188) onto card stock. Resting on a cutting mat, cut out the templates with a craft knife. Use a metal ruler to guide the knife.

6 Place the 3¼-in. wide pencil point template on a 3¼-in. wide pencil. Stick masking tape to the floorcloth along the three edges. Remove the template, leaving the masking tape in place, and repeat on the other 3¼-in. wide pencils, making the pencils different lengths.

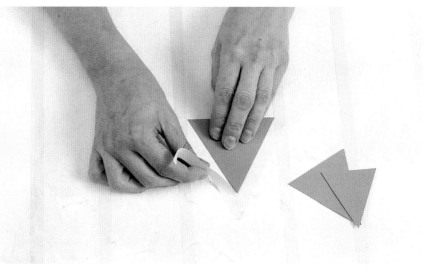

7 Repeat to mask off the points of the 2½-in. and 2-in. wide pencils, making them different lengths. Press all the masking tape down well.

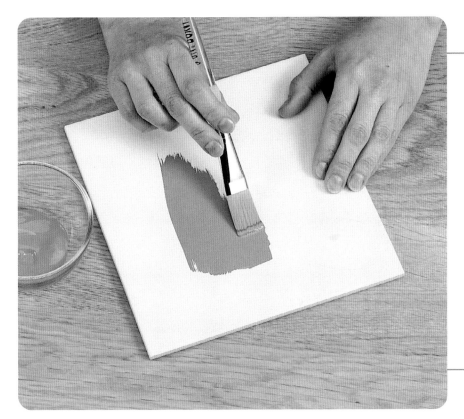

8 Apply a thin coat of gray acrylic paint to a ceramic tile or an old plate with the flat artist's brush.

9 Dab at the paint with a stencil brush and stencil one pencil, holding the brush upright and moving it in a circular motion. Hold a piece of cardboard along the masked edges while you are stenciling to prevent the paint straying beyond the masked edges.

10 Repeat, stenciling three of the other pencils with gray acrylic paint. With a clean brush, stencil the remaining pencils in black and shades of gray acrylic paint. Leave to dry.

11 Stick pieces of masking tape across all the pencils below their "points" and parallel with the long edges of the floorcloth. This is to mask off the "wood" of the pencils. Stick lengths of masking tape across each pencil tip to mask off the pencil "lead."

12 Blend white and gray acrylic paint together. Apply a thin coat of the blended paint to a ceramic tile or an old plate with a flat brush. Dab at the paint with a clean stencil brush and stencil the "wood" of the pencils.

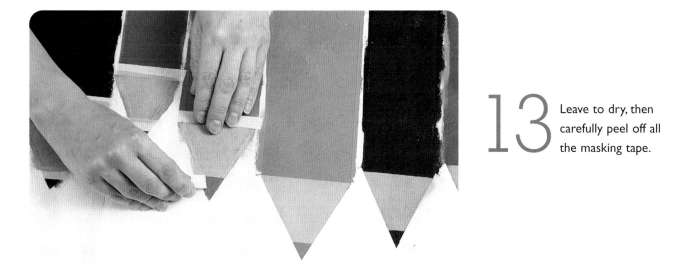

13 Leave to dry, then carefully peel off all the masking tape.

14 Apply three coats of clear water-based varnish to the floorcloth using the 3-in. paintbrush.

FREE AND EASY

Sometimes you simply do not want to be constrained by a stamp or stencil design. Perhaps you are not looking for a repeating pattern but yearn for the glamour of a stunning unique motif. Follow these handy tips, and you will quickly and effortlessly convert your dreams into reality. There are options here for all levels of ability and types of surface. So what are you waiting for?

Planning a design

1 You may have been inspired by an image you have seen in a book, on a billboard, or on your travels, but no matter how simple or complex the design, for successful results when painting freehand, sketching out the design is your best starting point.

2 If you want to transfer your design to a surface such as a wall or floor, plot out the design on graph paper first. If you are working in metric measurements, use a scale of 1:10; otherwise, a scale of 1:12 is best. When planning a design for a wall, take into account the position of doors, windows, light sockets, and power outlets, and mark them all on your graph paper. If you are planning a floor design, bear in mind the position of any large pieces of furniture.

Marking the design on the surface

Copying a sketch freehand

Once you have planned the design to scale, you need to transfer it to the surface you will be working on. If you feel confident of your abilities, you can copy your sketch freehand onto the surface using a soft pencil. Rub out any mistakes using an eraser.

Using a grid

Another alternative is to draw a grid over your chosen image and the equivalent grid, but on a larger scale, on the surface to be painted—usually a wall. So, for example, if you lay a piece of tracing paper over your image and cover it with a grid that is 3 squares deep and 4 squares wide, draw a grid of 3 squares deep and 4 squares wide on the wall using a soft pencil. Now draw the image onto the wall, copying what you see in each square on the tracing paper to each square on the wall. When you have finished, you can erase the penciled grid from the wall.

Using tracing paper

If you feel less confident, use tracing paper—or fabric transfer paper if you are working on fabric—to transfer your design. Start with a motif that you have enlarged to the required size. Trace the outline of the motif onto the tracing paper using pencil. Then simply turn the tracing paper over, lay it on the surface to be painted, and, holding it steady, pencil over the line again to give you a mirror image. If it is important that you do not reverse the image, for example to achieve a true representation of someone's thumbprint for the Toy Chest Thumbprint on pages 136–141, use the image in conjunction with graphite paper or turn the tracing paper over and pencil over the line again on the reverse side before transferring the traced image to the surface.

Keeping the hand steady

There are various designer tricks you can use to help keep your hand steady as you work and prevent wobbly lines.

Using a maulstick

Professional painters and sign makers use a maulstick—a stick with a soft, rounded, and padded head that you hold to act as a support for the working hand. Rest the head of the stick away from the working area, and then lean the working hand against the stick. This avoids resting your hand on the working area and smudging the paint.

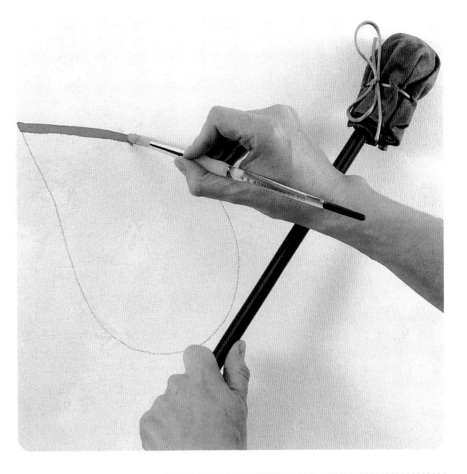

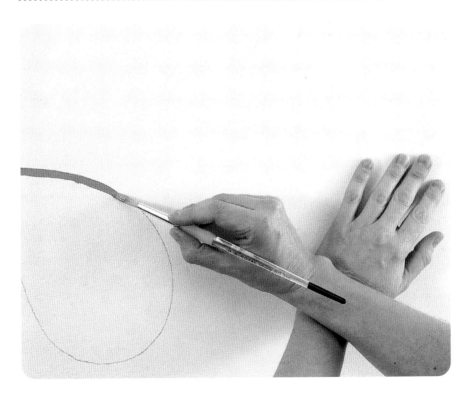

Using your hands

Simply resting the wrist of the working hand over the other wrist will help to steady your hand, too. Alternatively, you can hold the wrist or elbow of the working hand with the other hand. Another idea is simply to prop the elbow of the working hand on a handy piece of furniture or on a rung of a stepladder.

Circle artwork

Ever dreamed of being an artist? Well, this is your chance. Forget those pricey original artworks in the stores and paint your own. Color-match it to your room, and you're onto a winner!

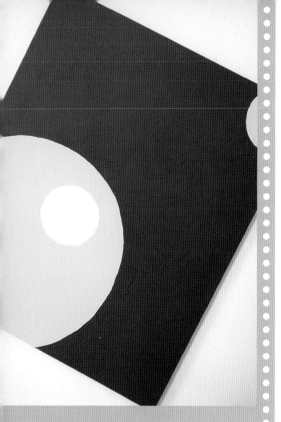

1 Position a bowl or plate in the bottom left-hand corner of the canvas so that it cuts into the canvas as far as you want, then paint around it with the artist's brush using the lime green paint. Leave to dry.

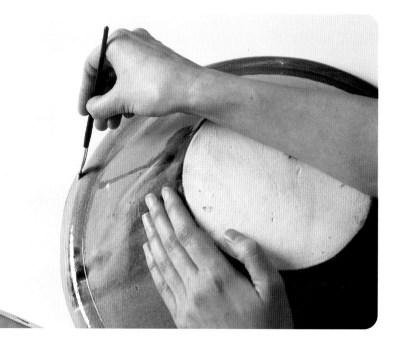

YOU WILL NEED:

- ready-stretched canvas
- large round bowl or plate
- size 2 artist's brush
- 1½ fl. oz. lime green acrylic or flat latex paint
- long steel ruler
- small cup or jar
- 1½ fl. oz. apple green acrylic or flat latex paint
- 1-in. paintbrush
- 2-in. paintbrush
- 1½ fl. oz. aubergine acrylic or flat latex paint
- ½-in. flat artist's brush

These quantities are for a canvas measuring 20 x 24 in.

2 Place a long steel ruler along the diagonal line running from top right to bottom left and place the small cup or jar along this diagonal, within the lime green arc. Remove the ruler and paint around the cup using the apple green paint. Leave to dry. Reposition the cup so that it cuts into the canvas at the top right-hand corner and paint an outline around it in lime green.

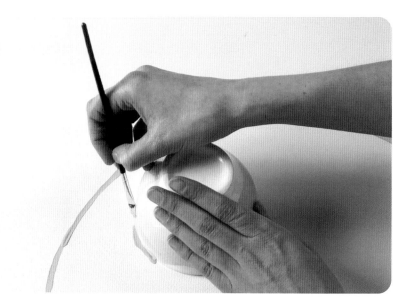

3 Using a 1-in. brush, fill in the large arc with the lime green paint and leave to dry. Paint a second coat if required. Paint the two small circles with the apple green and lime green paint and leave to dry. Paint a second coat if required. Use the 2-in. brush to paint the remaining canvas with the aubergine paint and leave to dry. Paint a second coat if necessary.

4 Paint the edges of the canvas using the flat artist's brush and continuing the relevant colors from the front of the canvas.

Tip
- Painting long, fast strokes gives a smoother line to the circles, but don't worry about getting the edges perfect—wobbly lines are quite acceptable.
- Wait until each circle is completely dry before painting the next to avoid color runs.
- You can use any color combination, but to play it safe make one color the same shade as your wall, one a couple of shades darker, and one a couple of shades lighter.

Painted plates

Fifties housewives loved the new motifs and colors that characterized postwar design. The black and white Homemaker china was especially popular. This design takes its inspiration from it.

YOU WILL NEED:

- paper
- felt-tip pen
- plain white china plates
- black outliner porcelain paint suitable for contact with food
- damp cloth
- black porcelain paint suitable for contact with food
- size 2 artist's brush

1 Plan out your design by doodling on paper with a felt-tip pen. If you have some fifties china as reference, so much the better. Keep your images simple, and limit them to the rim of the plate, as most porcelain paint manufacturers recommend that you do not cut directly on a painted surface.

2 Wash and dry the plates thoroughly before painting. Using the tube of outliner paint, carefully draw the outline of your motifs on the rim. Wipe away any mistakes immediately with a damp cloth.

3 Fill in the design using the artist's brush. Following the manufacturer's instructions, leave the plates to air-dry, then bake in the oven. Turn the oven off and leave the plates to cool in the closed oven.

Tip
- The paints used here are suitable for food use and are dishwasher-safe. However, check instructions carefully as brands can vary. Other paints may require varnishing or have different baking instructions.
- If you want to use more than one color, the second color can be applied almost immediately, as the paint dries in seconds.
- Odd plates for practicing on can be picked up cheaply at garage sales and thrift stores.

4 When you get more skilled, you can try more ambitious designs. If you are using several sizes of plates, complementary but different designs look good together.

Camouflage chest of drawers

Borrow from the world of fashion for a look that is bang up-to-date. Any teenager would be proud to show this chest of drawers off to friends. If you are feeling gutsy, camouflage a curtain or the wall behind, too, and just watch that chest vanish. Or, if you prefer, use grays and whites and go for snow camouflage instead.

YOU WILL NEED:

- chest of drawers
- medium sandpaper
- 3-in. and 2-in. paintbrushes
- 10 fl. oz. beige eggshell latex paint
- fine sandpaper and sanding block
- paper
- graphite paper
- card stock
- masking tape
- pencil
- cutting mat and craft knife
- ¼-in. and ¾-in. flat artist's brushes
- 5 fl. oz. each olive green, pale olive green, and mid-brown eggshell latex paint
- ¼ gal. clear matte water-based varnish

These quantities are for a chest of drawers measuring 40½ x 35 x 19 in.

1 Sand the surface of the chest and the drawer fronts with medium sandpaper to prepare them. Paint the chest and drawer fronts with beige eggshell latex paint using a 3-in. paintbrush.

2 Leave the paint to dry then lightly sand the surface with fine sandpaper and a sanding block. Apply a second coat of paint.

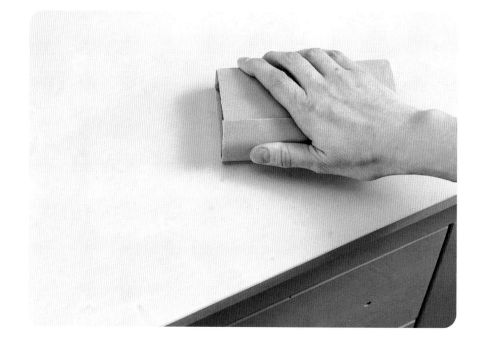

3 Enlarge the camouflage templates (page 187) to suit your chest of drawers. Tape a piece of graphite paper, graphite side down, onto card stock with masking tape. Tape the templates on top. Redraw the templates with a sharp pencil to transfer them to the card stock.

4 Remove the paper templates. Resting on a cutting mat, cut out the card stock templates with a craft knife.

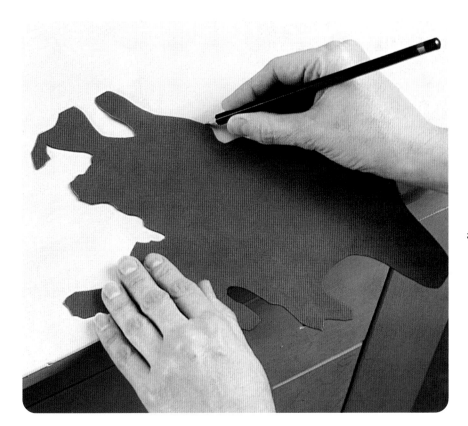

5 Place about half of template A on top of the chest and draw around it carefully using a soft pencil.

6 Fold the template over the edges of the chest to continue the design. Repeat to draw template A at random all over the chest and drawer fronts.

7 Paint the outline of one motif with olive green eggshell latex paint using the ¼-in. flat artist's brush.

8 Fill in the motif with the same paint and using the ¼-in. and ¾-in. flat artist's brushes. Repeat to paint all the motifs with the olive green eggshell latex paint. Leave to dry.

9 Draw around template B in some of the remaining spaces. Overlap the images already painted.

10 Paint these motifs with pale olive green eggshell latex paint as before and leave to dry.

11 Draw around templates C and D in the same way. Fill in any gaps and overlap the images already painted.

12 Paint these motifs with mid-brown eggshell latex paint in the same way and leave to dry.

13 Apply two coats of clear matte water-based varnish with a 2-in. paintbrush. Sand the chest and drawer fronts with fine sandpaper between coats.

Seedhead pillowcase

There is no need to spend money on fancy bed linen when you can make your own. This design of freehand-painted and sponged seedheads takes its inspiration from nature and is sure to bring sweet dreams. And the beautiful design lends itself to other surfaces, too. How about a painted seedhead panel on the bedroom wall to complement your linen?

YOU WILL NEED:

- pale pink cotton pillowcase
- paper
- pencil
- tracing paper
- dressmaker's pins
- masking tape
- fabric transfer paper
- plastic bag
- size 3 artist's brush
- 1½ fl. oz. blue fabric paint
- size 0 artist's brush
- 1½ fl. oz. dusky pink fabric paint
- ceramic tile or old plate
- ½-in. flat brush
- 1½ fl. oz. pale blue fabric paint
- small sea sponge

These quantities are for a pillowcase measuring 20 × 31½ in.

1 Wash and press the pillowcase to remove the dressing. Enlarge the seedhead template on page 188 to suit your pillowcase, then trace the template onto tracing paper.

2 Mark the positions of the seedheads evenly across the pillowcase using dressmaker's pins. Following the pictures above and on pages 126–27, mark the position of both the head and the stem of the falling seedhead.

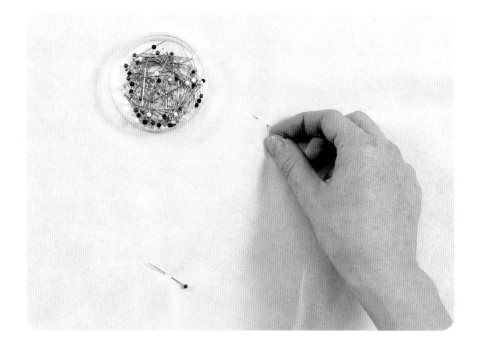

3 Use masking tape to tape the tracing onto the front of the pillowcase in the first marked position. Slip a piece of fabric transfer paper under the tracing, colored side down.

4 Redraw the seedhead with a sharp pencil to transfer the image to the pillowcase. Remove the tracing, then repeat for the other seedheads. Slip a plastic bag inside the pillowcase and smooth it out flat. This will prevent paint from soaking through to the back of the pillowcase.

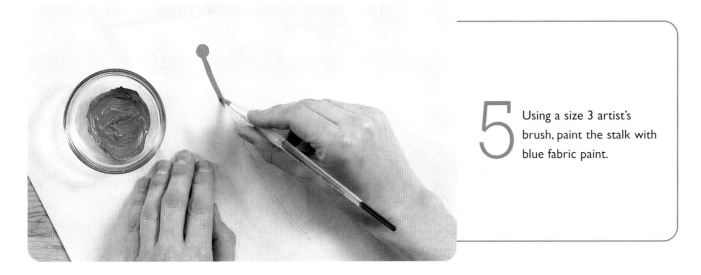

5 Using a size 3 artist's brush, paint the stalk with blue fabric paint.

6 Paint the seedhead in blue with a size 0 artist's brush, painting from the stalk outward.

7 Use the size 3 brush to dot the seeds at random around the edges of the seedhead.

8 Repeat on the next traced image using dusky pink fabric paint. Complete the next two images in the same way, alternating colors.

9 Paint some pale blue fabric paint onto a ceramic tile or old plate with a ½-in. flat brush. Use a small sea sponge to apply the paint in a 2-in. diameter circle around the pin that marks the head of the falling seedhead. Remove the pin to complete the sponging. Leave to dry then trace the falling seedhead over the sponging as in steps 3 and 4. Complete the seedhead in blue fabric paint as in steps 5–7.

10 Leave the paint to dry then remove the plastic bag. Following the paint manufacturer's instructions, press the pillowcase facedown to set the paints.

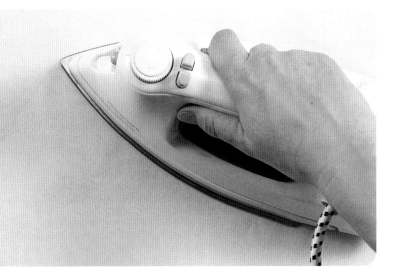

Circle floor

This painted floor imitates a circular rug but is rather more daring. Painting it in red on a pale wood floor against white walls looks very contemporary and is sure to be a talking point for your guests.

YOU WILL NEED:

- ball of string
- thumbtack
- scissors
- soft pencil
- fine sandpaper
- sanding block
- 10 fl. oz. bright red satin latex paint
- 2-in. paintbrush
- 5 fl. oz. clear acrylic varnish

These quantities are for a circle measuring 3 feet in diameter.

1 Decide on the diameter you want for your circle, taking into account the furniture in the room. Knot the end of a ball of string around a thumbtack and, holding the thumbtack lightly in the floor, unravel the string to the desired radius. Cut off the length of string and, holding it tightly, test the size of your circle.

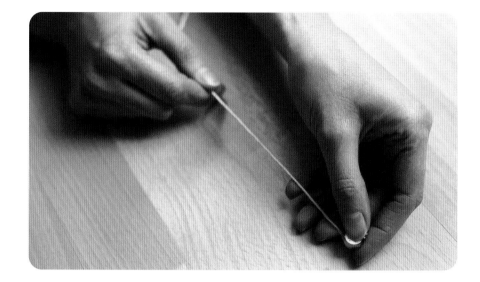

2 Hold a soft pencil very firmly at the end of the string, and, holding the thumbtack down firmly with the other hand, draw a circle with the pencil. Draw it in one fast, sweeping movement.

3 Lightly sand the floor surface within the circle using fine sandpaper and a sanding block. This provides a "tooth" to help the paint adhere.

Tip

• If your floor has already been varnished, you must first remove the varnish in the area being painted. Give it a thorough sanding and clean it with denatured alcohol.

• If you wish, you can use special floor paint instead of latex paint, but if you use it on a concrete floor, you must seal the concrete first.

4 Use the red satin latex paint and a 2-in. paintbrush to paint inside the pencil line. Leave to dry. Paint a second coat if required. Finish with a topcoat of clear acrylic varnish to protect the surface.

Toy chest thumbprint

Fingerprint your child to make a motif for a toy chest that shouts, "This is mine! Keep off!" Add a padlock, and their territory is truly staked out. And why stop at the toy chest? This idea works just as well on the door of their bedroom. "Intruders stay out!"

YOU WILL NEED:

- wooden toy chest
- medium and fine sandpaper
- 2½ fl. oz. quick-drying wood primer
- 10 fl. oz. red satin latex paint
- ink pad
- white paper
- scissors
- pencil
- black felt-tip pen
- masking tape
- graphite paper
- size 8 artist's brush
- size 5 artist's brush
- 5 fl. oz. black satin latex paint

These quantities are for a toy chest measuring 30 x 14 x 12 in.

1   Sand and prime the toy chest (see page 40). Paint it with two coats of red satin latex paint, sanding the surface with fine sandpaper between coats. Set aside to dry. Press your or your child's thumb onto an ink pad, then press the inked thumb onto a piece of white paper. Repeat a few times to create different strengths of image.

2   Choose the clearest image, cut it out roughly, then enlarge it on a photocopier to at least 200 percent to make it easier to copy freehand.

3 Copy the thumbprint freehand with a pencil onto a sheet of paper large enough to suit the lid of the toy chest. Go over the drawing with a black felt-tip pen, thickening up the lines as you go.

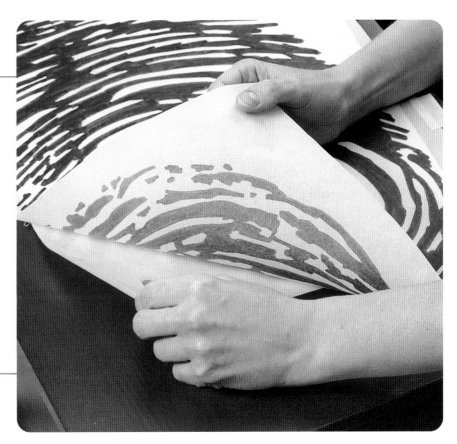

4 Tape the drawing right side up on the lid of the toy chest with masking tape. Slip a sheet of graphite paper facedown underneath.

5 Redraw the image with a sharp pencil to transfer it to the lid. Move the graphite paper if necessary so the entire image is transferred.

6 Starting at the center of the image, paint over the lines using a size 8 artist's brush with black satin latex paint. Use a size 5 artist's brush for the fine details.

7 Continue painting the thumbprint, working from the center outward. Leave to dry.

TEXTURE AND SHINE

Texture and shine techniques will take your paint effects projects to another level—from excellent to breathtaking. Add the texture of age, the shine of precious metal, or the frosted look of expensively etched glass. People have been doing it for centuries—no one will ever guess it is all trickery—and you will be amazed at just how simple it can be.

Crackle glaze

Crackle glaze produces a rather delicate effect. If you want a more pronounced, dramatically aged look, it is easy to cheat a bit. Rub some artist's oil paint—burnt umber is a good color to use—into the cracks using a soft cloth. This will give the cracks more emphasis and add an antiqued look to the finished piece.

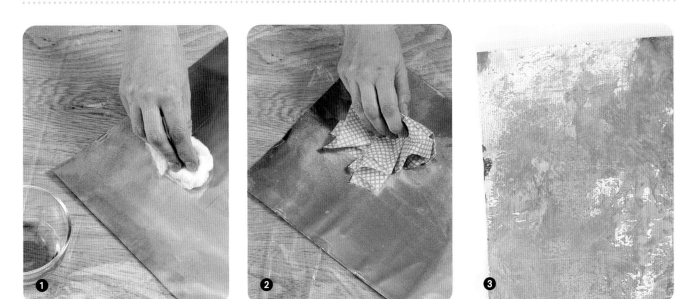

Verdigris

Verdigris is the patina or crust produced on copper, brass, or bronze when they are exposed to the atmopshere. You can use faux verdigris effects to give an appearance of age. We painted our two metal planters with latex paint to produce a verdigris effect (see pages 162–67). If you are actually working on copper, an alternative is to use one of the patination fluids that are on the market. These require less skill and give a very quick result.

❶ Start by cleaning the copper surface with denatured alcohol on a piece of cotton, then leave to dry thoroughly for two hours.

❷ Wearing a protective mask, apply the patination fluid with a piece of clean cloth.

❸ The copper will change color very quickly. Once you have the color you require, rinse the metal in water.

Weathered terra-cotta

This simple technique gives a lovely aged and weathered terra-cotta look to the most ordinary plastic. It looks especially good on items with classical-style detailing or molding, such as the plant pot used here.

1 Paint the plastic object with pale terra-cotta latex paint. While the paint is still wet, throw some dry builder's sand onto the surface.

2 Using a slightly damp sponge, apply some darker colored terra-cotta latex paint, making sure that you leave some of the paler color showing through.

3 Dilute off-white latex paint in the ratio three parts water to one part paint and brush it randomly over the surface.

4 Using a dry cloth, rub off some of the off-white paint. The plastic should begin to look dusty.

5 Finally, sponge a little turquoise latex paint over some areas to give a slight verdigris effect.

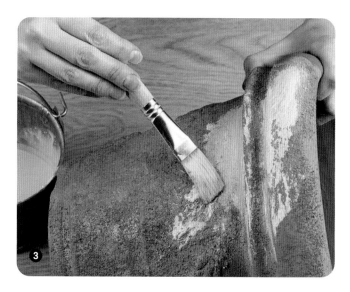

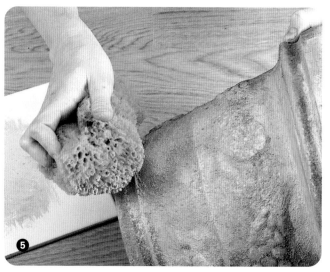

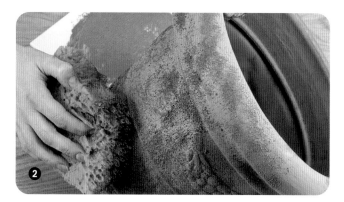

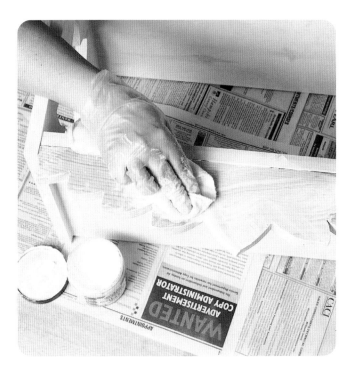

Liming wax

Liming is a technique used to lighten open-grained woods such as oak. It became popular with the arts and crafts movement of the nineteenth century, when there was a revival of interest in the whitewashed timber of the sixteenth and seventeenth centuries. You can achieve the look using wire wool and white latex paint, but liming wax is a pleasant-to-use alternative.

Sand the wood smooth, then remove any dirt and grease by wiping with a cloth dipped in mineral spirits. Wearing protective gloves, apply the liming wax sparingly with a cotton cloth, rubbing well into the grain with circular overlapping strokes. Then wipe across the grain with a clean pad, leaving the wax in the pores. After about ten minutes, remove surplus wax from the surface by gently polishing along the grain with a dry cotton cloth.

Glass frosting

❶ Using a stencil with frosting varnish enables you to apply a detailed, repeat design to a glass surface. Here, fix a star-shaped stencil to a glass bowl with masking tape and dab on the frosting varnish using a stencil brush.

❷ When the frosting is dry, remove the stencil and reposition as necessary.

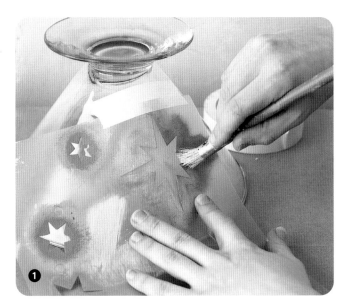

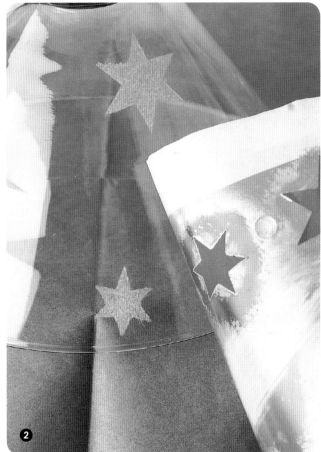

Rustic chair

If you have an attractive chair that's spoiled by old wax, varnish, or paint finish, this is an excellent way of giving it a rustic-style makeover. The materials you need to give an aged effect are simple—just some latex paint and special acrylic crackle glaze. By the time you have finished with it, your chair will look worn but well loved.

YOU WILL NEED:

- old chair
- steel wool or a rag
- denatured alcohol
- 1-in. paintbrush
- 5 fl. oz. off-white flat latex paint
- 5 fl. oz. acrylic crackle glaze
- 5 fl. oz. pale green flat latex paint
- paint can or other container
- a little raw umber artist's oil paint
- rag
- 2½ fl. oz. mineral spirits
- 5 fl. oz. oil-based clear matte varnish
- a little white artist's oil paint

These quantities are for an average wooden chair.

1 Prepare the chair by removing any old wax or varnish with steel wool or a rag and denatured alcohol. Leave to dry.

2 Using a 1-in. brush, apply a thin layer of off-white flat latex paint as an undercoat. Do not attempt to cover the wood with a completely opaque coat of paint. It will look better if the grain and any nicks and blemishes show through. Leave to dry for approximately five hours, then apply an even coat of acrylic crackle glaze with a clean brush and leave to dry overnight.

3 Using a clean brush, roughly apply a thick coat of pale green flat latex paint in as few strokes as possible. As the paint begins to dry, cracks will start to appear. These can be exaggerated by speeding up the drying process with a hair dryer. Leave to dry for five more hours.

4 Mix equal quantities of oil-based clear matte varnish and mineral spirits with a little raw umber artist's oil paint. Paint this mixture onto the chair a section at a time. Leave to dry for a few minutes, then wipe away any excess with a rag, leaving behind a brown "dirty" residue in the nooks and crannies. If you make a mistake, wipe the mixture away with mineral spirits before it dries and start again. Leave to dry overnight. Finish the chair with a coat of the oil-based matte varnish mixed with a small amount of white artist's oil paint to give it a dusty, aged appearance.

Shimmery glazed wall

This glamorous wall idea uses a shimmer-effect paint that contains minute metallic flakes. These give it a subtle, light-reflecting gleam. No one will ever guess how easy it is to do and how inexpensive— they are bound to think that you have had a chic interior designer at your beck and call.

YOU WILL NEED:

- graph paper
- pencil
- ½ qt. deep pink flat latex paint
- 4-in. paintbrush
- 2-in. masking tape
- level or plumb line
- 3-in. paintbrush
- 10 fl. oz. pink shimmer-effect paint

These quantities are for a wall measuring 108 square feet.

1 Plot your design to scale on a sheet of graph paper before you begin.

2 Paint the wall with two coats of deep pink flat latex paint using a 4-in. paintbrush, and leave to dry. Stick a length of 2-in. masking tape vertically down the wall where you intend the left-hand edge of the design to be. Use a level or plumb line to check that the line is straight.

3 Stick another length of tape at right angles to the first at the top of the tape. Again, check that the tape is level. Apply a second horizontal tape 32 in. below the first.

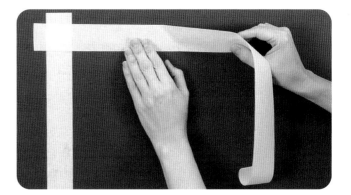

4 Run tape parallel with the vertical tape and 20 in. to the right of it to create a rectangle. Now stick two lengths of tape across the rectangle, dividing it into three sections. Press all the masking tape down well.

5 Referring to the manufacturer's instructions, paint the three sections with a shimmer-effect coat of paint using a 3-in. paintbrush. Apply the paint thinly near the masking tape so the paint is less likely to seep under any loose edges.

6 Leave the paint to dry, then peel off the masking tape.

Acid-etched mirror

Bring a touch of sophistication to any room with this stylish mirror. The project uses glass frosting spray, available from large hardware stores and artist's suppliers. It gives glass and mirror the look of having been expensively hand-etched or frosted—but at just a fraction of the cost.

1   Place the mirror upside down on a large sheet of plain paper and draw around it with a pencil.

2   Remove the mirror. Keeping within this outline, draw a rough oval shape to use as a stencil. Do not worry about making the oval too neat. Cut the oval out of the paper. Place the mirror right side up on sheets of newspaper. Working in a well-ventilated area, spray the paper stencil with repositionable spray adhesive or spray mount adhesive, leave it to dry for a few seconds, then press it firmly into position on the surface of the mirror.

YOU WILL NEED:

- mirror
- large sheet of plain paper
- pencil
- scissors
- newspaper
- repositionable stencil adhesive spray or spray mount adhesive
- glass frosting spray
- lighter fluid
- soft cloth

3 Holding the can of glass frosting spray about 6 in. away from the surface of the mirror, evenly spray the exposed area of the mirror. Apply two or three coats, then leave to dry.

4 Gently peel off the paper stencil. Any small marks can be easily removed with lighter fluid and a soft cloth.

Tip

• Always read the instructions on the can of glass frosting spray before commencing.

• The spray can be used on many glass objects, including wine glasses, windows, bowls, vases, and paperweights, but the finish is not dishwasher-proof.

• If you decide to have a mirror cut to order, have its edges beveled for a neater look.

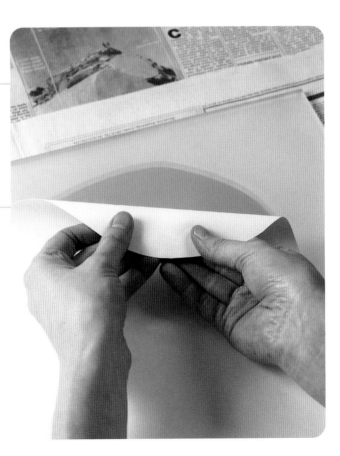

Mexican-style flowerpots

Patterns scratched into paint to decorate kitchenware have been used in Mexico since pre-Columbian days. The technique, known as *maque*, was originally worked into surfaces that had been lacquered with an oil or natural wax. The motifs used here are mischievous monkey characters found on clay stamps from Chiapas.

YOU WILL NEED:

- tracing paper
- pencil
- three square-section
  terra-cotta pots
- 1-in. paintbrush
- 2½ fl. oz. lilac flat latex paint
- potter's needle or awl
- 2½ fl. oz. orange flat
  latex paint
- 2½ fl. oz. green flat
  latex paint
- 2½ fl. oz. pink flat
  latex paint
- 2½ fl. oz. yellow flat
  latex paint
- high-gloss spray varnish

These quantities are for three
pots measuring approx. 4-in. high.

1 Trace the templates on page 184 and enlarge if necessary. Scrub the terra-cotta pots in soap and water to remove any dirt and dust. Leave to dry completely. Using a 1-in. paintbrush, apply a panel of lilac flat latex paint to the center of one side of a pot. Leave a ¼-in. border around the panel. Leave to dry for one hour.

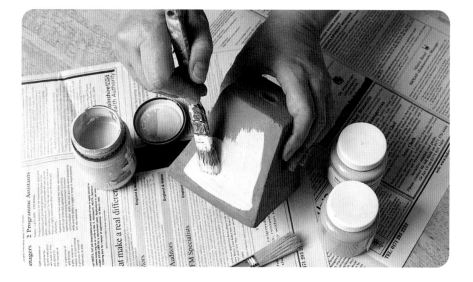

2 Using a potter's needle or awl, and with the traced templates as a guide, lightly scratch one of the images into the surface of the lilac paint. If you make a mistake you can paint over it. Once you are satisfied with the image, go over the lines with slightly more pressure, removing the paint a little at a time, until you get down to the terra-cotta surface. Widen the lines where necessary.

3 Using a clean brush, paint orange flat latex paint on the remaining sides of the pot and over the border surrounding the scratched, or scraffito, image. Paint the inside of the pot as well. If necessary, apply a second coat of paint once the first has dried. Leave to dry thoroughly.

4 Working in a well-ventilated area, lightly spray the entire pot with high-gloss varnish. Leave to dry. Repeat on the second and third pots using the other designs and the other paint colors.

Verdigris planters

Bring a touch of magic to a pair of simple metal planters—and with nothing more than some paint, brushes, and a sponge. Planters like these will add a stylish note and a touch of individuality to any patio or sunroom. Just add a hammock, lie back, and relax. Now where did I leave that cool drink?

YOU WILL NEED:

- two metal planters
- plastic sheeting or newspaper
- metal primer spray paint
- gold spray paint
- ½-in. and ¾-in. flat artist's brushes
- ceramic tile or old plate
- 5 fl. oz. dark aquamarine flat latex paint
- large sea sponge
- 5 fl. oz. light aquamarine flat latex paint
- 5 fl. oz. light turquoise flat latex paint
- paper towels
- 1½ fl. oz. off-white flat latex paint
- 5 fl. oz. clear matte oil-based varnish (optional)
- 2-in. paintbrush (optional)

These quantities are for two planters each measuring 13 in. high and 15 in. diameter.

1 Cover the surrounding area with plastic sheeting or newspaper to protect it from stray spray paint. Working in a well-ventilated area, spray the planter with gray metal primer to prepare the surface.

2 Leave the planter to dry, then spray it gold.

3 Apply dark aquamarine flat latex paint to a ceramic tile or an old plate with a ½-in. flat artist's brush.

Tip
● When spray-painting, apply a few light coats of paint rather than one heavy one, to prevent the paint from dripping.

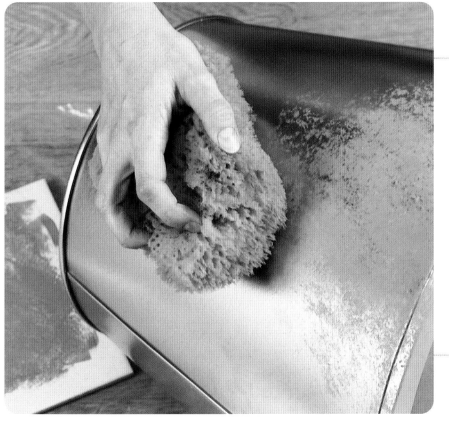

4 Moisten a sea sponge. Dab at the paint with the sponge, and sponge it at random all over one face of the planter. Work on one section at a time. It is not necessary to completely cover the surface: patches of gold can show through.

5 Sponge light aquamarine flat latex paint onto the planter in the same way. Blend the shades together with the sponge. There is no need for the dark aquamarine paint to dry first.

6 Pick up a little light turquoise flat latex paint with a dry ¾-in. flat artist's brush. Dab off the excess paint on paper towels.

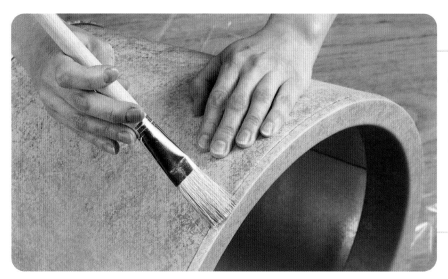

7 Brush the light turquoise paint lightly onto the edges of the planter to highlight them.

8   Set the planter aside to dry. Thin the off-white flat latex paint with a little water. Brush it onto one face of the planter with the ¾-in. brush.

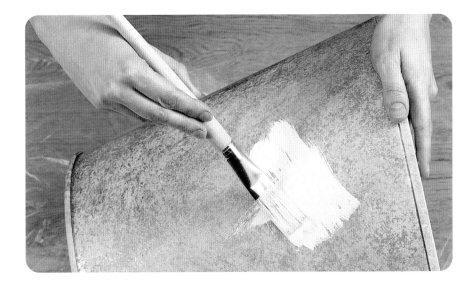

9   Rub the white paint off before it dries with paper towels, leaving some traces behind.

10   Cover the whole planter in this way, rubbing the white paint off before it dries. Leave to dry overnight. If you plan to use the planter outdoors, apply two coats of clear matte oil-based varnish with the 2-in. brush.

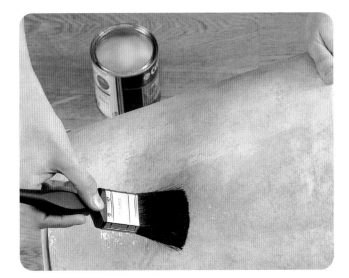

Waxed shelf unit

Here is an idea that protects as it glamorizes, and, what is more, you can make the colors as subtle or as strong as you please. I have gone for bold primaries, which makes the shelf unit a great choice for a child's bedroom. But you could choose a color mix of mustard, sage, and brown for a retro kitchen, or soft green, pink, and terra-cotta for a country-style bedroom.

YOU WILL NEED:

- three-tier wooden shelf unit
- medium sandpaper
- 2 tbsp. beeswax
- ½-in. squeeze of cobalt blue artist's oil paint
- paint palette or old container
- stick or brush for mixing
- soft cloth
- piece of cardboard
- cotton swabs
- ½-in. squeeze of cadmium red artist's oil paint
- ½-in. squeeze of emerald green artist's oil paint

These quantities are for a three-tier shelf unit measuring 28 x 10 x 10 in.

1 Thoroughly sand a three-tier wooden shelf unit with medium sandpaper to prepare the surface. Make sure you sand well into all the corners.

2 Mix a third of the beeswax with the cobalt blue artist's oil paint in a paint palette or old container, using a stick or the handle end of a brush to blend the mixture together. Add more paint and mix it in well if you would like a stronger color.

3 Using a soft cloth, apply the colored wax evenly into the recess of the top section of the shelf unit, on top of the unit, and on the upper surface of the top shelf.

4 Carry the colored wax over the front edge of the unit, using a piece of cardboard to mask off areas not being waxed.

5 Use a cotton swab to apply the wax into the corners and edges of the unit.

6 Mix beeswax with cadmium red artist's oil paint as before, and color another section of the unit using a clean piece of soft cloth and a cotton swab.

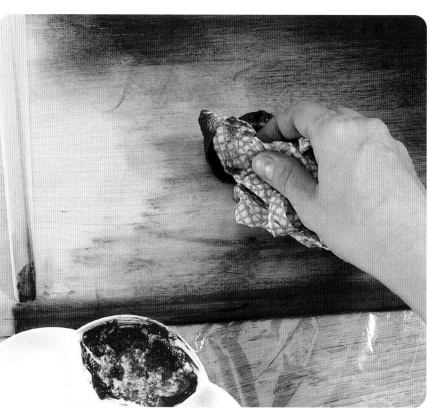

7 Repeat to color the third section and the base of the unit with beeswax colored with emerald green artist's oil paint.

8 Set the unit aside for 24 hours, then buff the surface all over with a clean soft cloth.

Frosted glass vase

This graphic frosted vase takes its inspiration from retro-style scraps of fabric featuring simple checkered and striped designs. The finished vase looks just as good empty as it does with a few simple blooms.

YOU WILL NEED:

- glass vase, 6 in. high and 8 in. wide
- cloth or paper to protect the work surface
- roll of 1-in. masking tape
- scissors
- glass frosting spray

1 For inspiration for your checkered pattern, look at retro-style fabric patterns featuring simple checks and stripes. Wash and dry the vase to ensure it is free from dust and grease.

2 Working on a table protected with a cloth or paper, and using lengths of masking tape, mask off those areas of the vase that are to remain clear. The pattern used here is a double row of frosted checkers above a wide frosted band. It appears on only one face of the vase.

3 Apply more masking tape firmly to the sides of the vase to protect them from stray frosting spray. Working in a well-ventilated area, apply the glass frosting spray in a gently sweeping movement, keeping the can at a distance of 6 in.

Tip

• Always read the instructions on the can of glass frosting spray before commencing.

• If there is any "bleeding" at the edges when you remove the masking tape, use a craft knife to scrape away the excess, taking care not to scratch the glass. Lighter fluid and a soft cloth can also remove mistakes; however, this tends to remove a lot of frosting.

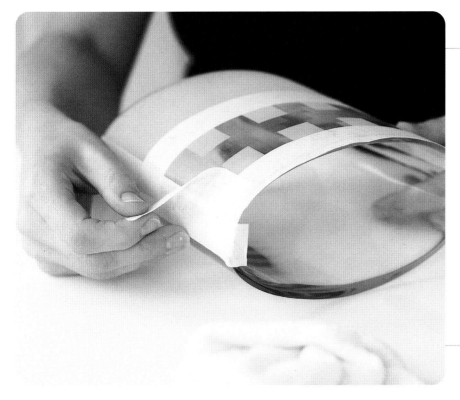

4 Leave the vase to dry for at least one hour, then carefully peel off the masking tape to reveal the frosted design.

Zen stripe

This simple-to-do vertical stripe of mottled color provides a strong accent to pale surroundings. Use it to enliven an otherwise plain white wall. Take care where you position the stripe, though—it will look most effective when placed approximately one-third of the way in from a corner, as shown here.

YOU WILL NEED:

- plumb line or level
- soft pencil
- colored masking tape
- 1-in. paintbrush
- 1½ fl. oz. blue flat latex paint
- paper towels or a clean cloth
- damp cloth
- 2-in. paintbrush
- 1½ fl. oz. ivory or off-white flat latex paint

These quantities are for a stripe on a wall measuring 9 feet high.

1 Use a plumb line or level to position two vertical lines on a white-painted wall, running from the baseboard to the ceiling, 1¾ in. apart. Mark the lines lightly with a soft pencil. Run masking tape—colored tape shows up best on a white wall—down the outer edge of each line to create an outline for the stripe. Dampen a 1-in. paintbrush slightly and dip it into the blue flat latex paint. Remove any excess paint by dabbing the brush on a paper towel or a clean cloth. Make sure the brush is quite dry, then, starting from the top of the wall, use light, downward strokes to paint the area between the strips of tape. Reload the brush as necessary to complete the stripe. Work quickly to cover the whole area before the paint dries.

2 Immediately after applying the paint, wipe the stripe with a damp cloth using downward strokes. This evens out the texture of the paint and removes some areas of color to create a subtle, patchy finish. Work the entire length of the stripe, reworking areas lightly to achieve the finished effect. Leave the paint to dry for a few hours, then remove the masking tape.

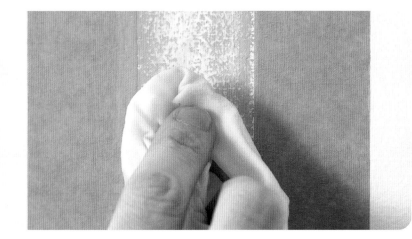

3 Measuring from the right-hand edge of the painted stripe, mark one vertical line ¾ in. away and another 8½ in. away. Mask off on the outside edge of these lines as before to create a second stripe slightly overlapping the painted blue one. Using a 2-in. paintbrush, apply ivory or off-white flat latex paint in the same way as in steps 1 and 2.

4 Remove all the masking tape while the paint is still wet to avoid lifting the paint from the wall. If the paint is left to dry first, it might be damaged when the tape is removed.

Tip
• Use masking tape along the baseboard and ceiling where the wall joins to protect them from paint.
• You may want to adjust the width of the stripes, making them narrower for a lower wall, and wider for a tall wall.

TEMPLATES

Above: Fern Stenciled Floor, page 54.
Enlarge to suit your floor design.

Left and above left: Leaf-Stamped Limed Floor, page 58. Enlarge to suit your floor design.

Above: Feather Curtain, page 86. Enlarge to suit your curtain design.

Above: Stenciled Numbers, page 66. Enlarge to suit your wall design.

Below and right: Mexican-Style Flowerpots, page 158. Enlarge to suit the size of your pots.

Below Funky Bathroom Wall, page 80.
Enlarge to suit your design.

Right: Shadowy Tree Room Divider,
page 70. Enlarge to fit your roller shade.

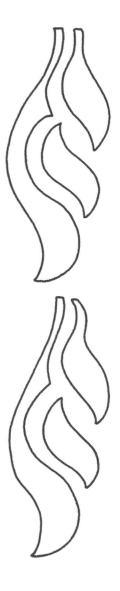

Above: Gilded Picture Frames, page 90.
Enlarge to suit your frame.

Left: Curling Scroll Wall, page 76. Enlarge
to suit your wall.

Below: Camouflage Chest of Drawers, page 118, shapes A–D. Enlarge to suit your chest of drawers.

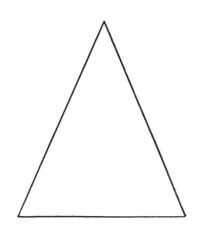

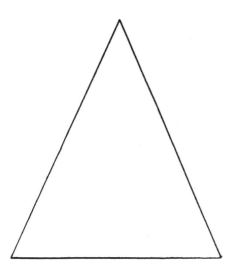

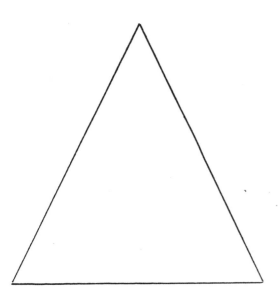

Above: Seedhead Pillowcase, page 126. Enlarge to suit your linen.

Left: Pencil Floorcloth, page 98, pencil points. Enlarge to suit your cloth.

ACKNOWLEDGMENTS

The suppliers

Thank you to the following companies who loaned props for the shoot:

Aston Matthews,
141–147a Essex Road,
London N1 2SN, England

Dulux/ICI Paint,
Wexham Road, Slough,
SL2 5DS, England

Flint Hire & Supply of London,
Queen's Row, London,
SE17 2PX, England
www.flints.co.uk

Paintworks Artists' Materials,
99–101 Kingsland Road, London
E2 8AG, England

The makers

Cheryl Owen
Shadowy tree room divider
Funky bathroom wall
Bathroom backsplash
Pencil floorcloth
Camouflage chest of drawers
Seedhead pillowcase
Toy chest thumbprint
Shimmery glazed wall
Verdigris planters
Waxed shelf unit

Sacha Cohen
Leaf-stamped limed floor
Checkered stamped floor
Curling scroll wall
Feather curtain
Gilded picture frames

Natalia Marshall
Stenciled numbers
Circle artwork
Circle floor
Acid-etched mirror

Marion Haslam
Fern stenciled floor
Painted plates
Frosted glass vase

Karin Hossack
Mexican-style flowerpots

Ali Hanan
Rustic chair

Jane Tidbury
Zen stripe

Picture credits

Page 11: © Kevin O'Hara/Powerstock.
Page 12: Bruno Perousse/Powerstock.
Page 13: Roger Viollet/Rex Features.
Page 14: © Superstock/Powerstock.
Page 17: Roger Viollet/Rex Features.
Page 19: © Michael Boys/CORBIS.
Page 25, 178–81: © Peter Aprahamian.
Page 29: © Doug Scott.
Page 23, 26, 28, 29: ©1998
Hollingsworth Studios, Inc.
Page 24, 25, 26, 27, 33: Olivia
Maynard.
Page 49, 50, 52–3, 58–65, 76–9, 86–9,
90–3, 143, 145: Lucinda Symons.
Page 54–7, 114–17, 174–7:
Sue Wilson.
Page 66–9, 110–13, 132–5, 146–9,
154–7: Chris Tubbs.
Page 145, 160–1: Ray Daffurn.

INDEX